Towards the Development of a Regulatory Framework for Polymetallic Nodule Exploitation in the Area

ISA TECHNICAL STUDY: No. 11

International Seabed Authority
Kingston, Jamaica

ISA TECHNICAL STUDY SERIES

A REPORT TO THE INTERNATIONAL SEABED AUTHORITY

PREPARED BY:

Allen L. Clark, Ph.D., Principal Investigator;
Jennifer Cook Clark, J.D., LL.M.;
Sam Pintz, M.Sc. Contributor

26 February 2013

NATIONAL LIBRARY OF JAMAICA CATALOGUING –IN – PUBLICATION DATA

Towards the development of a regulatory framework for polymetallic nodule
    exploitation in the area.

    p. ; cm. – (Technical study; no. 11)
    ISBN 978-976-8241-16-0 (ebk)

1. Ocean mining – Law and legislation
 2.   Marine mineral resources – Law and legislation
I. Series

341.455   – dc 23

International Seabed Authority
14-20 Port Royal Street
Kingston, Jamaica
Tel: (+1 (876) 922 9105, Fax: +1 (876) 922 0195
Website: www.isa.org.jm

Table of Contents

List of Acronyms

AGXI   Agreement relating to the Implementation of Part XI of the United Nations Convention on the Law of the Sea
APAL   Atmospheric Pressure Acid Leaching
BLM   Bureau of Land Management
BOT   Build-Operate-Transfer
CCZ   Clarion-Clipperton Zone
CHM   Common Heritage of Mankind
Co   Cobalt
COMRA   China Ocean Mineral Resources Research and Development Association
CoW   Contract of Work
CSR   Corporate Social Responsibility
Cu   Copper
DRC   Democratic Republic of the Congo
EMD   Electrolytic Manganese Dioxide
EMM   Electrolytic Manganese Metal
EMP   Environmental Management Plan
FoB   Free on Board
GATT   General Agreement on Tariffs and Trade
HPAL   High Pressure Acid Leach
HSB   Hybrid Social Business
IRR   Internal Rate of Return
ISA   International Seabed Authority
KP   Mining rights or authorization known as *kuasa pertambangan*
KMA   Known Mineral Area
LOSC   United Nations Convention on the Law of the Sea
LRMC   Long-Run Marginal Costs
LTC   Legal and Technical Commission
MMDA   Model Mining Development Agreement
Mn   Manganese
MSR   Marine Scientific Research
Ni   Nickel
NPI   Nickel Pig Iron
OECD   Organisation for Economic Co-operation and Development
PAL   Pressure Acid Leaching
PN   Polymetallic Nodule
PSC   Production Sharing Contract
ROI   Return on Investment
SIPP   Preliminary General Survey License
TPA   tonnes per annum
USGS   United States Geological Survey
WTO   World Trade Organization

Executive Summary

After decades 'on hold', there is renewed interest in the potential for commercial exploitation of deep seabed polymetallic nodules (PN). The principal drivers of this new interest are largely the result of five factors: a) a dramatic increase in demand for metal; b) an equally dramatic rise in metal prices; c) the high profitability of mining sector companies; d) a decline in the tonnage and grade of land-based nickel, copper and cobalt sulphide deposits; and e) technological advances in deep seabed mining and processing. Equally important is the impact of Papua New Guinea granting the first deep-seabed mining licene, in its territorial Bismarck Sea, to the Nautilus Mining Company of Canada. This has demonstrated that the private sector, and the financial institutions that support it, believe that deep seabed mining can be commercially viable.

In addition to the exploration contracts with the initial seven pioneer investors in 2001 and 2002, a second contract with Germany was signed in 2006. During the seventeenth annual session in 2011 the Seabed Authority Council approved the plans of work of Nauru Ocean Resources Inc. (NORI), sponsored by Nauru, and Tonga Offshore Mining Limited (TOML), sponsored by Tonga, for exploration for polymetallic nodules; and the plans of work of China Ocean Minerals Resources Research and Development Association (COMRA), and the Ministry of Natural Resources and the Environment of the Russian Federation, for polymetallic sulphides, in the international deep seabed (documents ISBA/17/C/2, 3, 4 and 5).

At the eighteenth annual meeting in 2012, an additional five applications were approved, bringing the number of active exploration contracts issued by the Authority to 17, compared to only 8 in 2010. The five new applications were made by: UK Seabed Resources Ltd. (sponsored by the Government of the United Kingdom of Great Britain and Northern Ireland); Marawa Research and Exploration Ltd. (a state enterprise of the Republic of Kiribati); G-TEC Sea Mineral Resources NV (sponsored by the Government of Belgium); and the Government of the Republic of Korea for manganese nodules, and IFREMER (sponsored by the Government of France) for polymetallic sulphides. In July 2012 the Authority received applications from COMRA and the Japan Oil, Gas and Metals National Corporation for exploration of cobalt-rich ferromanganese crusts.

Exploitation Framework - In recognition of these issues, and because the first contracts for PN exploration will expire in 2016, the Council of the International Seabed Authority (ISA) requested during its seventeenth session that the ISA Secretary-General prepare a work plan for the formulation of regulations for the exploitation of polymetallic nodules in the Area. This formulation is guided by Article 17 of Annex III, 'Rules, regulations and procedures of the Authority', which provides that the Authority "shall adopt and uniformly apply" regulations. Article 3, paragraph 5 of Annex III of the Convention provides that the regulatory relationship between the ISA and an operator shall be in the form of a contract obtained by approval of a plan of work.

Land-based regulatory regimes generally operate through a licensing process that in some jurisdictions is in lieu of contracts or in addition to contracts for reasons discussed below. This discussion will mainly refer to a licensing procedure and the ISA may wish to consider adopting a licensing procedure in addition to the approval of plans of work as a contract as part of its regulatory authority. In any case, in complying with this request, the ISA faces the challenge of developing an exploitation framework that ensures that PN exploitation will both: a) be for the benefit of "mankind as a whole" (including future generations); and b) foster commercially viable and sustainable exploitation (including reasonable economic returns) of the Area's mineral resources.

Exploitation - Based on available deep seabed nodule information, and experience gained from relevant land-based mineral developments, nodule exploitation and resource recovery can be expected to proceed sequentially from: a) relatively small but high-grade nodule areas with a rapid payback; to b) a limited, but significant, number of large and high-grade nodule occurrences; to c) similar sized deposits but of relatively low grade. It is very important that this model is progressively modified and monitored. A 'Whole of the Deposit' approach to nodule exploitation should be required that includes: a) a comprehensive resource and reserve assessment of the proposed mining area; b) the adoption of a sequential mining plan that maximizes reserve recovery, utilization and metal recovery; c) provision for periodic review and update of the mining plan; and d) performance guarantees and 'failure to perform' penalties, with the latter escalating over time to discourage behaviour inconsistent with approved mining plans, including the impermissible 'high grading' of the deposit, which is an all too frequent practice involving only mining the highest grade areas to maximize profits and minimize costs over the shortest period possible.

Regulatory Regime - The approach to the development of a regulatory framework for PN proceeds with an analysis of the factors that differentiate the regulation of deep ocean mining from its land-based counterparts. Some of the major issues of land-based regulation will translate to the regulation of PN exploitation. However, some issues (including the existing status of exploration, environmental issues, unique technical and logistical issues, the absence of traditional mine site communities and the relative strength and stability of the ISA as the regulator) will significantly differ and serve to change the focus, form and substance of the regulatory regime compared to that of a land-based regulatory regime. Some differences will result from shifts in the risks inherent in exploiting PN under the UNCLOS regime compared to those under land-based operations. The differences also provide insight into how the relative components of a

PN regulatory regime should be configured, and their relative 'weighting'. A predominantly statutory framework is suggested, to be developed along with a limited standardized contract to detail site, contractor- and sponsoring State-specific terms, based on the regulatory concerns and issues mentioned above.

Note: the present study does not deal with the specifics of an environmental regime for the exploitation of PN, as these issues are the subject of a parallel activity within the ISA, but it does specify key environmental components that will have to be developed and included in an overall exploitation framework. For example, environmental data will continue to be collected as part of an environmental monitoring plan during exploitation that will look at the environmental impact of exploitation, which is different to collecting environmental baseline data during limited sampling exploration. This will also require the analysis of all the environmental data collected to date to aid an understanding of the cumulative environmental impact of all aspects of exploitation. In addition, analysis of the data collected in the environmental monitoring programmes during exploitation will provide important feedback to (and perhaps inform modification of) the environmental monitoring plans and systems.

The factors that differentiate PN exploitation from land-based operations under single sovereign control (or more accurately, in modern times, under a hierarchical system of various national, provincial and local controls), and the inherent shifts in risk will also guide the substantive development of the regulations and steps in the licensing process. Most importantly, these differences and shifts in risk lead to the conclusion that a 'staged' or 'phased' licensing system for PN exploitation should be developed. It is suggested that, prior to the expiration of an exploration licence, the contractor (if interested in proceeding to the mining phase) be required to first apply for a *provisional mining licence based upon preparation and submission of a prefeasibility study and work plans to undertake a detailed bankable feasibility study based upon a pilot PN mining operation in the contract area.* The suggested validity of a preliminary mining licence is three years. The application for a provisional mining licence would include *inter alia:*

1. The technical, fiscal and environmental qualifications of the proposed operator.

2. Approved funding.

3. A prefeasibility study based on the contractor's previous exploration, transportation, processing and testing data, and analysis including an environmental impact assessment based upon the contractor's work during the exploration stage.

4. Plans of work for the term of the provisional mining licence including, *inter alia*:

    a. Plans for undertaking a detailed feasibility study based upon a pilot commercial site.

    b. Expenditure schedules.

    c. Development schedules.

    d. Mining methods.

    e. Production estimates for the pilot site during the term of the provisional licence and a tenured mining licence.

    f. Environmental management plans including closure and rehabilitation.

    g. Transportation and logistical specifics (including accident prevention) for the operation.

5. Performance assurances and guarantees.

6. Host and/or sponsoring government specifics.

7. Training and corporate social responsibility.

8. Size and area of concession.

The exact requirements of a prefeasibility study are included as a point of recommended future work.

Using information contained in the application for a provisional mining licence, including a prefeasibility study and environmental impact assessment, the ISA would be able (based upon a recommendation to develop an assessment methodology as future work) to determine whether the technical, environmental and economic analysis and conclusions reached would support the grant of a provisional mining licence to undertake a pilot commercial operation. If the pilot commercial operation is successful and a full detailed bankable feasibility study, including a full environmental assessment, indicates that a full-scale mining operation could be mounted and funded, the contractor could apply for a 'tenured' mining licence. An application for a tenured mining licence would include the data, information, analysis and conclusions of the detailed bankable feasibility study and full environmental impact assessment and proposed work plans. In turn, this would provide data, information and analysis allowing the ISA to determine (again, based upon a recommendation to develop an assessment methodology as future work) whether a full-scale mining operation could be undertaken in an acceptable and minimally environmentally invasive way.

It is suggested that an application for a tenured mining licence should include and be *conditional* upon:

1. Successful completion of the pilot commercial study under the provisional licence.

2. ISA approval of a detailed bankable feasibility study and full environmental impact study.

3. The technical, fiscal and environmental qualifications of the proposed operator.

4. Approved funding for the operation.

5. Plans of work for the term of the tenured mining licence including, inter alia:

    a. Expenditure schedules.

    b. Development schedules.

    c. Mining methods.

    d. Production estimates for the term of the tenured mining licence.

e. Environmental management plans including closure and rehabilitation.

f. Transportation and logistics specifics (including accident prevention) for the operation.

6. Performance assurances and guarantees.

7. Host and/or sponsoring government specifics.

8. Training and corporate social responsibility.

9. Size and area of concession.

In summary, a staged or phased licensing process, including the requirement of a prefeasibility study for a provisional licence, would allow the ISA to make an intermediate decision whether or not to allow a pilot project to fully demonstrate viability and safety, and the provisional licence would provide an important measure of control and power to claw back the project should unforeseeable problems arise, without having to suspend or terminate a full-scale mining project.

Other licensing options considered include types of exploitation licensing such as production sharing and contracts of work, and auctions for some blocks. The trade implications of the regulatory regime are briefly discussed and will be an interesting aspect to consider in developing the regulatory regime.

In developing a legal framework and its constituent components and functions, emphasis is based on finding the optimum fiscal balance to provide sufficient profitability, while identifying the threshold standards for environmental and mine health and safety. The development of the regulatory system will also help determine whether PN exploitation can provide sufficient returns to benefit mankind as a whole, and respond to the real and perceived environmental concerns, before full-scale mining can commence for PN and other resources in the deep ocean.

Fiscal Regime - While the fiscal framework for nodule exploitation is reasonably clear and consistent, it is not easily implemented and does not lend itself to definitive analysis. Three issues are particularly problematic: the setting of fiscal rates based on comparable land-based minerals; the problem of identifying tax and cost accounting codes on which fiscal calculations can be made; and the concept that a simple system can be developed that does not burden the ISA or mining investors. The overarching issue is that a royalty-based fiscal regime is faced with a number of fundamental, but in some cases incompatible, objectives. For example, a high degree of incompatibility exists between the objective of achieving economic efficiency and that of administrative efficiency. In terms of decreasing administrative efficiency, the most common royalties would be ranked as follows: a) unit-based royalties based on units of volume or weight; b) *ad valorem* royalties based on value of sales; c) hybrid royalties; and d) profit-based royalties. In contrast, in terms of economic efficiency, the ranking would be reversed. The selection of an appropriate royalty system is invariably a compromise between these objectives. The choice faced by the ISA, will be influenced by the size and diversity of the mining operations and the strength of the regulatory regime, which together will determine the degree of administrative complexity that can be accommodated without undue delay.

In addition, because exploitation will not be a public enterprise, questions immediately emerge about how to appropriately divide both profit and risk. These in turn raise difficult resource rent questions about capturing windfall profits and rents in the name of social justice. Both environmental destruction and the division of rent must somehow be accommodated in the eventual fiscal package.

Future Markets - Future Prices - Future Development - Nickel, copper, cobalt and manganese markets, prices and resource development are inescapably linked to global economic growth and the supply of, and demand for, these commodities. Present markets for nickel, copper, cobalt and manganese are demand driven, in large part by China and other Asian countries, and global supply is adequate to meet demand. For the intermediate term of 3 to 7 years, however, the demand for nickel and copper is expected to severely test the market's capacity to respond because of both decreasing deposit grades and the time required to bring new capacity on line. For the longer term of 7 to 10 years, it is anticipated that the demand for nickel, copper and possibly cobalt and manganese may exceed supply unless significant new land-based deposits are discovered, or alternative sources such as the deep seabed polymetallic nodules of the Area are exploited.

Corporate Social Responsibility (CSR) - It is proposed that the ISA, with inputs from industry and developing nations, considers the development of a Hybrid Social Business (HSB) model for industry that explicitly sets an expectation that corporate social responsibility for operations in the Area will simultaneously pursue two objectives: a) specific positive social impacts and returns; and b) specific baseline financial returns. The HSB model is a significant modification of the traditional business model, which only incorporates general levels of CSR. In this respect, it differs from the more pure Social Business Model of Yunus (2010) and others that focused primarily on non-profit industries.

The HSB model may be of particular interest to the ISA in terms of addressing the 'Lost Benefits' issue:

1. First and foremost the concept explicitly addresses the 'dual challenge' issue in that the corporation will fund/assist specific programmes that will be of value to all mankind, for example, the sustainable development of deep seabed

resources to preserve the marine environment and to reduce poverty while meeting the return on investment (ROI) requirements of investors.

2. Secondly, and more specific to the ISA, the HSB model is directly applicable to supporting the extant ISA Endowment Fund for Collaborative Marine Scientific Research on the International Seabed (MSR) programme (ISA, 2008a and b, Lodge, M., 2008).

3. From a market perspective, an HSB company programme has significant appeal to many potential investors and shareholders (particularly diversified portfolio investors) who wish to invest in socially responsible corporations.

The linkage of HSB and MSR with issues directly relevant to the Area as well as with developing nations' local, national and coastal management activities represents a win-win opportunity for the ISA, industry and developing nations and it is strongly recommended that the ISA address this issue as part of both the regulatory and fiscal regime for PN exploitation.

Conclusion and Recommendations - The potential for PN, polymetallic sulphide and cobalt-rich manganese crust exploitation within the Area is arguably higher now than at any other time in history. This impending reality requires that the ISA, as essentially the 'Mining Ministry of the Area', must quickly prepare to meet this rapidly evolving challenge. Meeting this challenge requires that a strategic framework be developed that allows the ISA to have in place the necessary mandates, organizational capacities (technical and administrative), policies and regulations (implementing rules and regulations) and capacities (fiscal, manpower and specialties). The following is an attempt to broadly identify the major organizational, fiscal and research recommendations that must be addressed, over the next 3 to 5 years, as part of an overall strategic plan to ensure that the ISA can meet the challenge.

Organizational

The ISA considers the development of an internal Mining Inspectorate with the specific responsibilities of maintaining oversight and compliance with all exploration and exploitation licence activities. This would specifically include a 'Mining Registry', a 'Compliance Office', a 'Data and Archive Center' and an 'Inspector General's Office'. There are many different administrative models but for efficiency, capacity and security a separate operating unit would be advisable. Such a responsible agency does not presently exist within the ISA, which in accordance with the evolutionary approach to its establishment reflected in the 1994 Agreement, has been principally geared up as an international organization providing meeting services to member States and expert bodies. However the present high level of interest, coupled with the need for many operators to apply for exploitation licences by 2016, indicates a critical need to begin detailed discussions for the funding, planning and implementation of such an 'administrative agency' capacity within the ISA in the near future. In addressing this need it is recommended that the ISA undertake a comparative analysis of representative administrative agencies as a basis for the development of a similar capacity within the ISA. Such capacity would need to include transparent funding mechanisms, whether through cost-recovery or an alternative basis, secure data management and analysis, maintenance of a mining claims registry to international standards (ISO 4001) and financial and accounting capacity.

The ISA forms a permanent committee to address the clear and urgent need to rationalize and incorporate past and present environmental rules, regulations and requirements with, and within, the evolving exploitation frameworks for PN and other metal resources within the Area. This is logically an LTC function but there needs to be transparent engagement with the deep-sea mining industry and other stakeholders in this process. The real concern is that: a) this process is not viewed as an ad hoc activity but as a critical component of whatever 'responsible agency' ensues; b) working groups and committees serve as a defined interface for environmental regulations for both prospecting and exploitation; c) there is a 'competent' body providing continuity across differing resources (polymetallic nodules, polymetallic sulphides and cobalt-rich crusts; d) the process identifies and addresses environmental issues as they might arise; and e) the process would become a permanent part of the 'responsible agency'. More importantly, it is argued that it would benefit the ISA if industry recognized that there was a formal, continuing and identified group monitoring their activities.

The ISA undertakes a study specific to the development of a set of unified and common operating procedures, as is done within most on-land mining Ministries and Agencies, for the evaluation, licensing and monitoring of PN, cobalt-rich manganese crusts and polymetallic sulphides prospecting, exploration and exploitation.

Fiscal

1. Ensure that whatever resource rent process is employed is:
   a. Simple.
   b. Equitable.
   c. Transparent.
   d. Defensible.
   e. Responsive to change.
2. Monitor to ensure that: a) the ISA receives its fair share of 'resource rents' after deductions; and b) that host country commercial policies do not give an unfair advantage to the commercial exploiter of the resources.
3. Monitor the 'transactional' part of the mineral-processing portion of the 'mine-to-market' chain, to ensure that all transactions are 'arm's length' and closely reflect prevailing market prices for metals. This will be particularly critical with respect to any royalty-based resource rent capture scheme ultimately adopted.

Research and Study

1. The development over the next 3 to 5 years of an overall framework of activities for the ISA, in conjunction with potential PN developers and member countries that will establish the internal ISA structure and capacity to manage PN exploitation in the Area.

2. Conduct a component analysis of a tax-like infrastructure (incorporating rules, procedures and administrative staff, audits, legal decisions etc.) for determining project profits and ensuring that optimum resource development and financial flows are achieved.

3. Undertake a cost-benefit analysis to determine the sensitivity levels for fees and costs associated with PN exploitation.

4. Undertake an evaluation by tax professionals, with international experience and knowledge of the special characteristics of mining, and of the issues, framework and applicability of business tax code for PN development within the Area.

5. Undertake framework studies specific to the following areas of PN exploitation activities:

   a. Monitoring and compliance.
   b. Resource recovery, utilization and valuation.
   c. Creation of implementing rules and regulations for legal regime.
   d. Structure of an Environmental Mining Plan.

6. Conduct definitional meetings to reach concurrence on the structure and requirements for:

   a. Pilot mining.
   b. Prefeasibility study metrics.
   c. Classification of resources and reserves specific to seabed mining.

1. Programme Background

Introduction

The last decade has seen a tremendous worldwide expansion of social and economic development, and with it a corresponding increase in the demand for minerals and energy. This economic growth and demand for metals continues to be of growing concern in terms of: a) the supply of critical metals, for example, gold, copper, nickel and cobalt; and b) the increase in the price of metals. As a result of these concerns there has been a shift of exploration and development expenditure to 'non-traditional' mineral sources, for example, polymetallic nodules (PN), seafloor massive sulphides and cobalt-rich ferromanganese crusts, occurring within and beyond the territorial waters of individual nations.

In light of this rapidly expanding interest in both increased exploration and commercial exploitation of deep seabed resources, the International Seabed Authority (ISA) has recognized the need to develop a provisional framework for the commercial exploitation of the polymetallic manganese nodule resources of the deep ocean. The framework is not intended to be overly prescriptive and is formulated to enable sufficient flexibility to be suitable for a wide range of situations and information levels (such a framework will be generally applicable to the exploitation of seafloor massive sulphides and cobalt-rich manganese crusts).

The scope of work for the present International Seabed Authority (ISA) consultancy was developed and undertaken with the guidance of the Secretariat. The principal components are broadly to:

1. Review the applicable provisions of the United Nations Convention on the Law of the Sea (UNCLOS) (United Nations, 1982), the Agreement on the Implementation of Part XI of the Convention (United Nations, 1994) and related materials.

2. Review relevant existing and proposed regulatory regimes for land- and marine-based development for commercial norms and precedents that might provide guidance and inputs for the establishment of seabed nodule mining regulations.

3. Provide guidance on policies for exploitation based on an analysis specifically encompassing: the long-term market for PN metals (nickel, copper, cobalt); a sensitivity analysis of PN economic studies; and an assessment of alternative metal supplies (laterite nickel deposits).

4. Define and assess the impact of applicable economic (taxation, debt financing, payments to the authority), legal (national and international norms and requirements) and administrative issues (national requirements on sale and use of resources).

5. Provide inputs on the following three specific, related and overarching issues:

   a. How to provide for sustainable development of the nodule resources while optimizing both the 'Common Heritage of Mankind' (CHM) and the return on investment (ROI) for the developers.

   b. What are the optimal and permissible level of 'resource rent' that should accrue to the Authority.

   c. What should be the composition (fees/taxes/rents/profit sharing) of those rents?

6. Define the scope and content of an 'internationally acceptable' framework for a feasibility study.

7. Arrive at a document for presentation to the Legal and Technical Commission in 2013.[1]

The consultant worked at ISA headquarters in Kingston, Jamaica between April 30, 2012 and May 4, 2012. Work was coordinated by ISA Legal Counsel Michael Lodge and detailed discussions were conducted with Mr. Lodge; Senior Legal Officer Kening Zhang; Marine Geologist Vijay Kodagali and other ISA staff.

In undertaking the consultancy the basic enabling documents relevant to the exploitation of deep seabed minerals included: the Agreement relating to the implementation of Part XI of UNCLOS; the ISA implementing 'Regulations on Prospecting and Exploration for Polymetallic Nodules in the Area' (ISA, 2000); and, outside the ISA, a vast range of studies (developmental, economic, legislative and regulatory) related to land-based mineral development.

Background

As has been noted by many practitioners, agencies and authors, the mining of deep seabed PN has been 'on hold' for decades as a result of several factors, particularly low and fluctuating commodity prices and the resulting uncertainty about long-term economic viability, and a variety of technologic issues. However, during the first decade of this century five separate issues have rekindled an interest in the exploitation of PN resources.

Specifically, the late 1990s and early 2000s saw two major economic changes that had a direct and dramatically favourable impact on potential PN exploitation: a) dramatic increases in metal demand; and b) an equally dramatic rise in commodity prices.

Similarly, three non-economic issues arose that, although more indirect, were equally important in terms of potential PN development. The first was Papua New Guinea's granting of the first deep seabed mining licence, in its territorial Bismarck Sea, to the Nautilus Mining Company of Canada (Nautilus Minerals 2011). This was particularly important because it provided a 'prototype system' (legal, administrative, fiscal, environmental and social) for deep seabed mineral exploitation (albeit at lesser depth than most PN resources in the Area).

Second, and related to the issuance of the mining licence, was that the Nautilus Corporation demonstrated that: a) a viable and acceptable mining plan, meeting all national economic, social and environmental regulations could be developed; and b) although much of the technology is unproven under real-life operation, the project's initiation demonstrated that the private sector, and the financial institutions that support it, believe that deep seabed mining can be commercially viable.

Third, in addition to the exploration contracts with the initial seven pioneer investors in 2001 and 2002 and a second contract with Germany in 2006, the Authority signed additional contracts during the seventeenth annual session in 2011 with Nauru Ocean Resources Inc. (a company sponsored by the Government of Nauru) and Tonga Mining Offshore Limited (a company sponsored by the Government of Tonga) for PN exploration, and with China Ocean Mineral Resources Research and Development Association (COMRA) and the Government of the Russian Federation for polymetallic sulphide exploration. At the eighteenth session in 2012 an additional five applications - by UK Seabed Resources Ltd. (a company sponsored by the Government of the United Kingdom of Great Britain and Northern Ireland); Marawa Research and Exploration Ltd. (a state enterprise of the Republic of Kiribati); G-TEC Sea Mineral Resources NV (a company sponsored by the Government of Belgium) for manganese nodules and the Government of the Republic of Korea; and IFREMER (sponsored by the Government of France) for polymetallic sulphides - were approved, bringing the number of active exploration contracts approved or issued by the Authority to 17, compared to only 8 in 2010. Most recently, in July 2012, the Authority received applications from COMRA and the Japan Oil, Gas and Metals National Corporation (JOGMEC) for exploration of cobalt-rich ferromanganese crusts within the Area.

In recognition of these issues, and because the first contracts for PN exploration will expire in 2016, the ISA, during its seventeenth session, requested that the ISA Secretary-General prepare a work plan for the formulation of regulations for the exploitation of PN in the Area.

Assumptions for the Study

The following assumptions underlie the development of this study:

1. The PN resources of the Area are to be exploited for the good of mankind as a whole within a regulatory framework "similar to that of land-based regimes" to be defined by the ISA.

2. All entities applying and working under the exploitation regime will be State or private entities organized under a member State's corporate law.

3. All PN exploitation within the Area will be conducted within the framework of existing, and to be executed, ISA policies and procedures for PN Exploitation (it is presumed that the PN exploitation regime will be a template for future regulation of the exploitation of other minerals).

4. Resource exploitation within the Area will be conducted utilizing industry best practices and standards.

5. The ISA will have free and open access to all relevant information required to ensure full compliance by contractors both within and outside the Area.

It is recognized that there are inherent uncertainties and issues associated with these assumptions and they are addressed within the study.

Notes
1.
The present report will not deal specifically with the development of an environmental framework for nodule exploitation, as this area will be part of a separate ISA programme. Therefore, the report does not discuss regulation of environmental impact assessments or environmental management plans except to make provision for their incorporation into exploitation regulations

2. Issues of Polymetallic Nodule Development

Introduction

The formulation of a discussion related to resource recovery and resource utilization of the PN resources of the deep seabed must be within the guiding principles of CHM (UNCLOS 1982) and for peaceful purposes. These concepts were further defined under Article 136 of the United Nations Law of the Sea Treaty (UNCLOS) in 1982 as related to "the seabed and ocean floor and subsoil thereof, beyond the limits of national jurisdiction." By extension, it can be argued that there are four core components (Frakes, J., 2003) of CHM that govern PN exploitation, resource recovery and utilization, of the deep seabed:

1. There can be no private or public appropriation; no one legally owns common heritage spaces.

2. Representatives from all nations must manage resources contained in such a territorial or conceptual area on behalf of all, since a commons area is considered to belong to everyone; this practically necessitates a special agency (ISA) to coordinate shared management.

3. All nations must actively share with each other the benefits acquired from exploitation of the resources from the common heritage region. This requires restraint on the profit-making activities of private corporate entities in accordance with the concept of a global public good.

4. The commons should be preserved for the benefit of future generations, and to avoid a 'Tragedy of the Commons'[1] scenario.

Although the CHM sets forth the overarching framework for deep seabed mineral exploitation, the actual implementation is broadly defined by the 1994 Agreement on the Implementation of Part XI (sections 6 and 8 of the Annex) as follows:

1. Section 6, on production policy, emphasizes that the development of the resources of the Area shall take place in accordance with "sound commercial principles", that "there shall be no subsidization of activities in the Area", and that "there shall be no discrimination between minerals derived from the Area and from other sources."

2. Section 8, paragraph 1, on financial terms of contracts, provides that:

   a. The system of payments to the Authority shall be fair to both the contractor and to the Authority and shall provide adequate means of determining compliance by the contractor within such system.

   b. The rates of payment under the system shall be within the range prevailing in respect of land-based mining of the same or similar minerals in order to avoid giving deep seabed miners an artificial competitive advantage or imposing on them a competitive disadvantage.

   c. The system should not be complicated and should not impose major administrative costs on the Authority or on a contractor. Consideration should be given to the adoption of a royalty system or a combination of a royalty and profit-sharing system.

   ...

   e. The system of payments may be revised periodically in the light changing circumstances.

The Dual Challenge

The ISA, as the agency responsible for

defining and overseeing deep seabed mineral exploitation, faces the obvious and complex challenge of developing an exploitation framework that ensures PN exploitation is simultaneously: a) for the benefit of all mankind and future generations (social); and b) fostering commercially viable and sustainable exploitation (economic) of mineral resources in the Area. Understanding and resolving the dual challenge is dependent on three issues: a) resource recovery (how much); b) resource utilization (when); and c) resource sustainability. Underlying all of these considerations is the transition of the Area's PN resources to reserves (Figure 1).

Figure 1:   The Resource-Reserve Classification

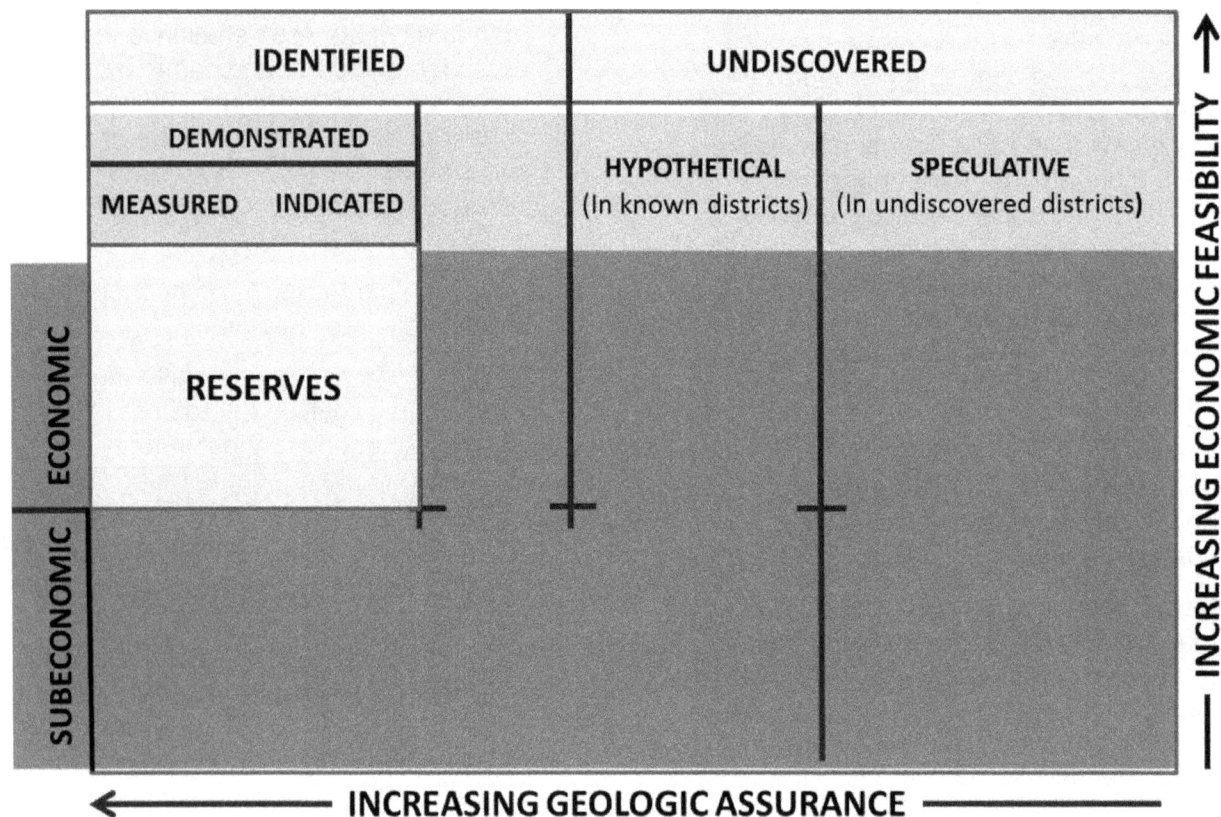

(USGS/USBM, 1980)

Within the mining sector mineral occurrences are normally classified in terms of the certainty of economic potential as 'Resources' or 'Reserves'.[2] At present all PN occurrences in the Area would be classified as identified sub-economic resources because of the requirement to be economically minable.

Nevertheless, with additional sampling, analysis and pilot mining and processing, many of the resources of the more maturely explored areas could be more quickly transferred to economic reserves. The economic necessity of physically demonstrating that any given potential mine site has adequate reserves to support a viable mining operation is a primary determinant of the economic viability of a deposit.

Issues of resource (reserve) recovery - The Area Resources - It must be emphasized that a 'viable and bankable' PN mining enterprise has yet to be conclusively demonstrated, as available resource information is based on: a) the very limited number of areas that have explored in detail; b) large areas with limited exploration; and c) the vast majority of the Area remaining largely unexplored in terms of

Issues of Polymetallic Nodule Development

nodule distribution and grade. In 2010, the ISA published a comprehensive assessment of the manganese nodule resources expected to occur in an approximately 5 million km^2 area of the Clarion-Clipperton Zone (CCZ), and concluded that the CCZ may host more than 27 billion metric tons of manganese nodules, containing approximately 7 billion metric tons of manganese, 340 million metric tons of nickel, 290 million metric tons of copper and 78 million metric tons of cobalt. Although the resource estimate is by any standards 'huge' the fact remains that 80 to 90 per cent of the resources of the Area would be classified as 'hypothetical' or 'undiscovered' resources with unknown economic potential.

The role of the Private Sector - The primary role of industry is to identify, within the resources available, that portion of the resources that are commercially viable, i.e. the reserves. On land, approximately 1 of every 1,000 prospects available would have adequate reserves to be commercially mined. If viewed in the context of the resources of PN occurrences within the Area, it is likely that only a small percentage of the licence area (approximately 10 to 15 per cent) will have commercially viable reserves. More importantly, minable reserves are scattered throughout a mine site. However, such areas are: a) usually spread throughout the 'mine site'; b) have a high abundance of nodules (approx.14kg/m^2); and c) are often associated with obstacles to mining.

To be economically viable, mining will have to be selective and efficient, which means that only a limited portion of any given mine site may be exploited before the 'miner' moves on to the next mine site. Although this approach is both common and appropriate on land, where more comprehensive mining is possible due to ease of access and efficiency of operations, this may well not be the case within the Area. This issue is discussed later in the section.

Potential resource development - The following discussion is based largely on present knowledge of, and what can be inferred from the identified and sub-economic PN resources of the area. Analyses show that neither the tonnage nor the grades of nodules are evenly distributed regionally or locally, as is the case in large on-land mineral provinces such as the Ural Mountains or the Andes. This comparison is critical in terms of addressing the resource recovery issue of the Area.

Specifically, it is expected that within the Area, based on terrestrial experience, nodule exploitation and resource recovery will proceed sequentially as follows:

1. Because of the high risk associated with virtually any pioneering mining endeavour, it is anticipated that initial nodule mining will be focused on relatively smaller but comparably high-grade nodule areas affording a rapid payback.

2. There will be a limited, but significant, number of large and high-grade nodule occurrences of sufficient tonnage and grade to be economically viable at a large scale.

3. Mining and processing technology is developed and scalable to 'mine level' operation. There will be a 'larger number of smaller but equally high-grade deposits' representing longer-term development possibilities as mining and processing capabilities improve in scale and capacity.

4. In the longer term it is expected that additional, similar sized deposits of lower grade will be defined and potentially exploited.

Mine site resource-reserve recovery - If the short- to long-term assessment of potential mining enterprises in the Area is reasonably accurate, initial exploitation will undoubtedly and appropriately (from a commercial perspective) be focused on those areas of highest nodule density and grade. *The overarching concern for the ISA is to avoid unduly selective 'High Grading' (mining only the highest density and quality areas) of individual mine sites.* Therefore, the maximization of resource recovery requires that the ISA ensure that exploitation proceeds with a 'whole of the deposit' mining plan that provides for the maximum recovery of economically exploitable nodules of various grades, and not just the highest density and highest quality nodules, over the life of a defined mine area.[3] Key issues relating to ability of the ISA to ensure maximized reserve recovery include:

1. Comprehensive resource-reserve assessment of the proposed mining area that includes:

   a. Validation of 'Measured' and 'Indicated' reserves.

   b. Evaluation of 'Inferred' resources.

   c. A defined sequential mining plan for all reserves that includes maximization of reserve utilization.

   d. Metal recovery.

   e. Periodic review of the mining plan with special emphasis on recovery optimization.

   f. Performance evaluation within a defined set of Evaluation Metrics.

   g. 'Failure to perform' penalties.

   h. Penalties should escalate with the severity of non-performance.

Trace Metals - Some 3 per cent of the 'average' manganese nodule is made up of the primary economic metals nickel (1.4 per cent), copper (1.2 per cent) and cobalt (0.6 per cent). PN also include trace amounts of molybdenum, tellurium, titanium, zirconium, lithium and rare earth elements (REE) such as neodymium, lanthanum and ytterbium (Hein, 2012, Mukhopadhyay, R. *et. al* 2008)). However, it must be emphasized that the recovery of some metals (particularly heavy REE, even in trace amounts) may constitute a relatively small, but significant economic benefit of PN exploitation. This possibility is being actively investigated by contractors and followed closely by the Authority.

Conversely, the presence of certain trace elements may in some cases, as occurs with many on-land deposits, be an economic disincentive with respect to a nodule exploitation project if processing and refining penalties are incurred because of their presence in the ore or concentrate. For the foreseeable future the trace amounts of contained metals are classified as an identified and non-economic resource.

Resource conservation - A major problem associated with most deep-ocean mineral resources is that of resource conservation. Because of their inherently difficult location on the seafloor it is expected that: a) it will be very difficult to achieve optimal levels of PN recovery (from a total resource perspective), within a given deposit area; and b) dilution of the ore will be a problem in marginal areas of any deposit.

Another major potential problem in the mining of PN deposits is the economic necessity of 'high-grading' the deposit. This will be particularly true if the operational costs of mining are very high, which could necessitate mining only the highest grade portions of the deposit. Economically, this can be viewed simply as mining a deposit with a high cut-off grade. However, because of the particular circumstances that surround the mining of deep ocean resources it may not be feasible, as it often is on land, to assume that the reserve can be revisited for recovery at a later date. This may represent both a serious technical and perception problem in terms of ISA's CHM responsibilities.

Notes

1 The 'tragedy of the commons' is the depletion of a shared resource by individuals, acting independently and rationally according to each one's self-interest, despite their understanding that depleting the common resource is contrary to their long-term best interests.

2 A 'mineral resource' is accepted as meaning a concentration of material of intrinsic economic interest such that there are reasonable prospects for eventual economic extraction. The characteristics of a mineral resource (including location, tonnage, grade, continuity) are estimated from geologic evidence and knowledge, such as exploration samples from drill holes. Mineral resources are subdivided into 'measured', 'indicated' and 'inferred' categories, in order of decreasing geologic confidence. An 'ore reserve' is defined as the economically mineable part of a measured or an indicated mineral resource. Its assessment includes mining, metallurgic, economic, legal, environmental, social and governmental considerations, such that the extraction can be reasonably justified. Ore reserves are subdivided into 'proved' and 'probable', in order of decreasing financial confidence.

3 Because of variation in minable reserves, metal content and grades, and variable processing recovery standards and guidelines will be project-dependent and therefore included in the proposed mining plan. However, exploitation legislation should contain regulations requiring reporting, specific to the reserve utilization and metal recovery portion of the mining plan.

3. Developing a Legal Framework for Exploitation of Deep-Sea Polymetallic Nodules

Overview

The process of developing a regulatory framework for the exploitation of PN is a legal, technical and good governance exercise to determine how best to capture optimal benefits to mankind as a whole from mining, while imposing a rational and realistic regulatory regime upon operators[1] that will allow mining with only the highest quality mining, social, environmental and fiscal practices. The analysis requires an understanding by all stakeholders that investors can only operate within the economic reality of externally set commodity pricing, and requires internal rates of return sufficient to justify the exploitation operation. These parameters set practical limitations on regulatory authority that nation States, especially developing nation States, often do not understand. This lack of understanding almost invariably results in less than optimal regulatory regimes that discourage the highest quality operators and bypass the associated higher levels of socio-economic development and environmental protection that they can provide. It also tends to attract and encourage poorer quality operators and illegal practices.[2] In almost every case a poor regulatory regime tends to skew operator behaviour and either restricts or inhibits the optimal return of benefits, potentially resulting in social and environmental problems.

Anticipating these problems, UNCLOS (United Nations, 1982) and the Agreement relating to the Implementation of Part XI (United Nations, 1994), hereinafter called 'AGXI', require the ISA to capture optimal benefits from resource development and to set high thresholds for responsible mining practices, especially for the environment, pursuant to the precautionary principle and mine safety and health. As the field of deep-sea mining slowly progresses to the commercial exploitation stage, the ISA as regulator needs to craft a sharply defined regulatory regime for PN mining. The challenge is to bridge the historically difficult divide between acceptable commercial return on investment while not hindering progress or unintentionally encouraging behaviour that decreases the overall value of the resource, and to mandate, monitor and enforce the safe development of a truly frontier endeavour.

The major contrasts between deep ocean mining versus land-based mining that will impact upon the development of a regulatory regime for PN exploitation are expected to be, *inter alia*:

1. Generally, the geological risk of development will tend to be lower than most land-based mining because the resource potential of concessions has been studied extensively and is already recognized (even if not yet quantified as a resource).

2. The amount of data and information concerning PN exploitation is relatively great compared to similar resources for a land-based project since there are already baselines for the work, especially in terms of the environment. This will hopefully allow for better analysis at the various licensing stages than is the case for most land-based mining projects.

3. So far, the companies and States that are interested in pursuing projects appear to be developing specific ocean and deep sea technology to mine PN nodules, whereas the substandard technical quality and ability of operators are often key concerns for governments in land-based projects, although it can be anticipated that the quality of operators and mining practices will always be a key concern.

4. Illegal mining of PN by other, non-licenced operators, traditionally a huge concern for regulators, will be limited due to access and technical limitations.

5. Similarly, small-scale mining, also traditionally a huge concern for regulators, should not be an issue.

6. Infrastructure requirements are vastly different for deep ocean mining than for land-based projects - perhaps being more closely related to offshore oil and gas infrastructure (ocean conditions, open water facilities and equipment, and transportation). This will require far less integration into the many and varied sectors of land-based infrastructure, for example, roads, camp and mine site development and communication.

7. Operators will presumably only need to work with the ISA and not many levels of local, regional and national authorities that invariably pose extreme political risk for land-based operations; entailing fewer licences and permits and fewer taxes and fees. The 'regulatory' variables for operators working with the ISA and a host or sponsoring country appear to be far fewer.

8. Operators will presumably not need foreign investment insurance in the traditional sense unless it is needed for processing, transport or sale within a nation State's territory, or for conducting business under the auspices of a sponsoring government; although this issue has yet to be addressed.

9. The singular type of resource extraction for PN nodules will allow for a more tailored regulatory approach than a regulatory approach, which needs to consider factors including different types of commodities, mining operations, transportation and processing, as in land-based regulatory regimes.

10. Traditional mine site communities for PN extraction do not exist, so one of the most contentious and potentially risk-laden areas for a mining project does not exist for the ISA. However, the ISA is responsible for creating a benefit stream to developing country constituents that will satisfy the UN community.

The traditional political (as opposed to technical and environmental) risks facing operators would appear fewer for deep-sea mining. An exception could be political risk in a company's relationship with a host or sponsoring nation that may wish to realize economic or other benefit from the PN mining operation. This issue has not been explored extensively. It is anticipated, however, that host and sponsoring countries will want to realize some gain from PN exploitation. While deep seabed mining will not provide for much infrastructure development, employment or other traditional benefit streams, there will be value-added gains from the downstream mining operation, especially if processing is undertaken in a host or sponsoring State.

Aside from requiring host and sponsoring nations to provide effective oversight over a company undertaking deep-sea mining activities, there is little guidance under the UNCLOS regime as to the legal relationship between a company and sponsoring State. Unlike land-based mining, a State will not have *in rem* jurisdiction over the PN resource, which would presumably preclude claims for imposition of royalties; however, it may seek to impose taxes or other obligations upon a company. The multinational nature of other types of businesses and its obligations to home and host governments is fairly well understood, but not at all in the case of deep-seabed mining. For example, many modern countries have double taxation treaties with one another to preclude two jurisdictions taxing the same entity twice. Similar concerns may be present here.

In addition, and importantly, the extent of a State's jurisdiction over the activities of the mining operation itself is not totally clear in relation to the potential overlap between the obligations of the State to oversee the company's activities and ISA's regulatory mandate. In many developing countries, issues involving corporate ownership and control often have serious impacts on mining regulators when questions of ownership and control over the mining operation arise. Moreover, additional thought should be given to the expected benefits - or lack thereof - to a host or sponsoring State's role in PN exploitation. Some of these issues may be considered in regulations concerning State certification. However, these are areas that will certainly merit additional consideration in the development of a regulatory regime for PN exploitation.

Some other risks also appear to shift significantly to the ISA for example, the 'social' risk in terms of providing benefit streams for development to its UN constituency. Also, although the costs and risks of operating a deep sea mining operation will not be fully known until in place and hard-won experience has been garnered, it appears that costs (other than those for mounting the mining operations and related transportation), might be significantly less because regional infrastructure does not have to be developed, and there is less need to deal with the numerous layers and sectors (communications, transportation, resource procurement, employment) of the local, regional and multiple ministries of a national government.

In this general context, the following discussion will consider some of the more important issues in developing a deep-sea PN exploitation legal and regulatory regime.

Enabling Environment and Authority

Initial considerations will focus on the UNCLOS enabling environment, which is already familiar to the ISA and which will include, *inter alia*:

1. Delineating the scope of ISA's authority specifically regarding the PN exploitation regime.

2. Defining the respective components of the regulatory regime to include regulations, contracts, licences and the relationships between them.

3. Expressing ISA's authority to contract and with whom.

4. Defining the legal relationship between the ISA and operators, contractors, States, sponsoring States, and other third parties.

5. Reserving authority to 'manage' and 'safeguard' PN resources by issuing licences and permits, and to monitor, inspect and enforce the regulatory regime.

6. Powers to make additional rules, regulations and procedures, including emergency cease and desist orders and the power and resources to immediately direct adequate resources to a given area under its control.

7. Authority to implement the PN exploitation regime.

In short, the ISA will need to reserve for itself substantial power and authority to manage, regulate and oversee the exploitation regime based upon the principles of:

1. High sensitivity to environmental concerns and use of the precautionary principle.

2. Highly technical and as yet unknown challenges associated with successful deep ocean mining.

3. Obligation to preserve and to direct benefit flows to the developing world.

4. Actively demonstrating good governance.

5. Maintaining the reputation of the UN as a fair, independent and competent regulator.

Article 17 of Annex III, 'Rules, Regulations and Procedures of the Authority' provides that the Authority "shall adopt and uniformly apply" regulations. Article 3, paragraph 5 of Annex III of the Convention provides that the regulatory relationship between the ISA and an operator shall be a contract obtained by approval of a plan of work.[3] On-land regulatory regimes generally operate through a licensing process that in some jurisdictions is in lieu of contracts or in addition to contracts for reasons discussed below. This discussion usually refers to a licensing procedure, which the ISA may wish to consider adopting in addition to the approval of plans of work as a contract as part of its regulatory authority.

The form, scope and constituent parts of a conventional regulatory regime will need to be prescribed through a concise and transparent statutory framework of regulations, some areas of which are prescribed in Article 17 of Annex III. Other issues that the ISA may wish to consider include, *inter alia*:

1. Who may apply for a PN exploitation licence (provisional mining licence or tenured mining licence)?

2. Status of existing concessions.

3. Priority, preference and security of tenure.

4. Exact procedures and requirements for applying for a PN exploitation licence.

5. Components of an acceptable plan of work.

6. ISA response requirements.

7. Minimum standard of performance for mining, operations, environmental considerations and mine health and safety, for example, vessel safety, underwater operations and salvage operations.

8. Reporting requirements.

9. Self- and third-party monitoring and assessment of performance.

10. Fiscal requirements.

11. Corporate social responsibility and governance.

12. Closure and rehabilitation.

13. Administrative resolution of disputes prior to resorting to formal dispute resolution under the Convention for contractors, ISA and third parties.

14. International trade implications.

15. If necessary, and not provided elsewhere, delineation of an adequate

internal administrative structure and capacity within the ISA to implement the PN exploitation regime including an independent registrar, cadastre, resource assessment databases, other administrative and reporting processes and procedures.

16. *Force majeure* and its definition.

17. Other obligations under other international law and conventions.

18. Other technical legal issues such as severability and interpretation.

Underpinning the above issues surrounding: a) enabling the regulations; b) scope and authority of the ISA; and c) composition of the regulatory regime, are the legal relationships between the ISA, the Enterprise, an operator or contractor and other third parties. In the previous Exploration Regulations, the ISA chose to adopt a short standardized contract and provide the bulk of the regulatory provisions in the Exploration Regulations. With regard to PN exploitation, the scope of the regulatory provisions and the types of relationships and contracts for commercial exploitation will require the ISA to determine again what kind of bilateral legal relationships it will have and what split is appropriate between statute and contract. In addition, multilateral contracts might be considered if the ISA requires additional assurance from States that they are providing the legal framework and means for contractors to comply with the Convention and contracts.

Composition of Regulatory Framework

Generally, the least mature regulatory regimes tend to regulate mining via negotiated agreements on a case-by-case basis (for example, Central Asian Republics, the transitional economies of South East Asia). As the regulatory regime matures and the structure and capacity of the regulator improves, the regime tends to move towards a statutory minerals or mining code or law (for example, Australia, Canada, Botswana, Chile, Papua New Guinea). Sometimes, a standardized agreement to govern project-specific or site-specific issues is also prescribed in the legislation (for example, the previous Indonesian CoWs).

The question of 'how much' should go into a mining code as opposed to being included in an agreement or contract is governed by issues including:

1. Regulator maturity, capacity and structure.

2. Importance of and differences between project and site-specific issues.

3. Relative stability of agreements and legislation under the relevant legal regime.

4. Ease of monitoring and administration of each.

5. Enforcement issues - legal authority to enforce statutes versus enforcement of contract terms, breach and remedy issues.

6. Whether there are sufficient checks and balances in terms of regulatory authority, statutory process and controls, contractual processes, controls and mechanisms, administrative law processes and mechanisms (including dispute resolution).

These factors are not generally based on the subject or substance of the provisions, but rather the capacity, procedures and instruments available to the regulators.

It is understood that the ISA is considering whether a model contract such as the Model Mining Development Agreement (MMDA) could be used for PN exploitation. One of the major concerns with contracts governing mineral exploitation is the government's (or in this case, the ISA's) power to suspend or terminate a licence if it is granted pursuant to a contract. Depending on how well the contract or agreement is drafted and regulatory power is reserved, a licence may or may not be suspended or terminated without significant government liability until the issue is referred to international arbitration or litigation. Other issues

surrounding the use of agreements for PN exploitation will concern ISA's limitation of liability. As a result of these and other concerns, the more mature and technically capable regulatory authorities have pursued more comprehensive statutory frameworks for comparative ease of management, reservation of regulatory power and limitation of liability. Properly drafted, these issues can be incorporated into contracts. However, the regulator still faces risks associated with the interpretation of the contract by third parties in contrast to the broad interpretation of permissible regulatory authority under statute.

Interests Surrounding Contracts in a Regulatory Regime

There is no question that the mining industry needs clarity, consistency and stability in a regulatory regime. Because of this, industry tends to prefer negotiated contracts, especially with less mature regulatory authorities, as these are perceived as providing the most stability over the life cycle of the project. The recent MMDA is a good example of a project by predominantly (though not entirely) industry-oriented groups designed to encourage the use of mining development agreements. In the absence of a comprehensive, rational statutory regime with a stable track history that allows adequate return on investment for the risks taken, operators will prefer to:

1. Negotiate a total package of their obligations to ensure profitability over time.

2. Ensure options to transfer, convey, pledge or mortgage project interests.

3. Ensure the security of terms and conditions (stabilization) over time.

4. Force negotiations over any changes or developments.

5. Where possible, choose a dispute resolution forum and choice of law.

International finance and investment guarantee organizations also tend to prefer negotiated contracts with less mature regulatory regimes so:

1. Security interests are protected.

2. Regulatory authority to suspend, modify or halt the project is circumscribed.

3. A preferred method of dispute resolution is specified.

However, many of the issues listed above are not present in the conventional UNCLOS regime. Indeed, unlike many sovereign governments (especially of developing and transitional governments), the ISA has a stable history and track record and is likely to remain stable for the foreseeable future. Its goals are clear and agreed upon by all member countries. It has the ability to formulate a fair, efficient and effective regulatory regime (unlike many sovereign regimes that are subject to political agendas or lack the political will or technical knowledge to do so). Also, importantly, AGXI requires uniformity of terms and conditions to be applied to all contractors pursuant to the mandates of equality of treatment. This is greatly enhanced by the ISA practice and procedure of coordinating expert and public consultation. This will be especially important for the formulation of exploitation regulations to preclude later claims that some stakeholders have not been heard, or that industry was able to negotiate terms and conditions that did not provide adequate benefits for mankind as a whole, or that some companies received more favorable treatment than others.

Despite this, legitimate site- and project-specific elements will exist for deep-sea PN exploitation that the ISA or Enterprise may wish to incorporate into a standardized form agreement.

Types of Agreements

Various types of contracts would appear possible (though probably not all are equally desirable) under the Convention and AGXI, including, *inter alia*:

1. Development and production agreements.

2. Joint venture agreements, especially for the Enterprise (per UNCLOS and AGXI language).

3. Production sharing agreements.

4. Contracts of work.

5. Build-operate-transfer agreements.

6. Service contracts.

Each of these entails a slightly different legal relationship between the regulator and contractor and there are pros and cons to each. Some of these agreements may actually be more amenable for deep-sea mining than traditional land-based mining, such as production sharing (the relative economics of which are discussed elsewhere) or even a contract of work, perhaps for the Enterprise.

The major types of agreement that governments enter into concerning mineral resources include:

Concession or lease agreement – generally a grant of use of land in return for revenue including, royalties, taxes and fees:

1. An exclusive right to use a specific area to explore, develop and mine.

2. Title to or ownership of minerals generally stays with government or until a defined point of recovery.

3. Certain period of time.

4. Controls major terms and conditions of relationship.

5. Can be based on a model (usually country-specific) or individually negotiated.

6. A government is not usually involved in the project or production of the commodity although it can demand an equity stake.

Pros: A concession agreement is the most straightforward to administrate. If structured correctly it can maximize government return and subject the investment to the most practical government oversight, especially when the government has regulatory capacity constraints.

Cons: Government (especially centrally-planned, transitional and developing) often believes that a concession agreement does not give it enough control over the project and does not provide enough economic return. Concession agreements are variously known by other names such as:

1. Mineral investment agreements
2. Mineral lease agreements
3. Mining agreement
4. Development agreements
5. Mineral Exploration and Production Agreement

Usually concession agreements accompany minerals legislation and often include provisions for the relationship between the agreement and the minerals legislation. The best examples of concession agreements include: Lao PDR; Chile; Tanzania; Botswana; Australia; and Papua New Guinea.

Service contracts - usually an agreement between a government and a contractor where the project is controlled by the government. The company is a contractor hired to undertake the work. The contractor is responsible for exploring, developing and producing but it does so under the 'service contract' to be paid for their services out of the profits of the project.

Pros: The government retains control of the project and title to the minerals.

Cons: Not enough stability for investors and often not enough return. There is no transfer of mineral title and the project cannot be assigned, transferred or alienated. It is not often used in the international minerals industry. It is similar to Build-Operate-Transfer (BOT) in other industries.

Hybrid systems - These usually start as service contracts because the government wants to control the project, but in order to induce companies to undertake the project various aspects of a concession contract are incorporated. Examples include the Philippine Financial and Technical Assistance Agreement and the Indonesian Contract of Work (CoW). On the face of the contracts, they initially appear to be 'service contracts' but they are a hybrid of service and concession contracts with special provisions to provide stability and an adequate return for investors. The most important factors underlying the CoW's relative success for Indonesia (both in terms of attracting investment and generating government revenue) was two-fold:

1. It created (within each 'generation' of CoW) certainty concerning the terms and conditions that would apply over a project's life (terms would not be subsequently renegotiated).

2. The investment regime (the mining law with its system of exploration permits - SIPP and KPs for smaller areas and CoW for larger areas) guaranteed that a company undertaking exploration could, if it were successful in locating an economic mineral deposit, continue to the development and mining stages with a CoW.

It is often asked whether the Indonesian CoW was successful. If 'success' is judged by the amount of exploration generated, resulting mining and revenue generated to the government, the answer is yes, as billions of dollars have been generated from mining. Industry generally views the CoW system as very successful because companies were able to work in the past under a relatively stable regulatory regime. However, if success were determined by whether the CoW was able to stand the 'test of time' and provide a high level of development for Indonesia, the answer would be inconclusive. Since 1997, the implementation of the CoW has been extremely problematic for a variety of economic and political reasons. The existing (and latest) generation of CoW in Indonesia is a seventh generation document

Developing a Legal Framework for Exploitation of Deep Sea Polymetalic Nodules (an eighth was considered but never put into place). Seven or eight generations of a contract should indicate that the original CoW met with only limited acceptance (in this case, limited acceptance by the government). Also, arguably, the original CoW's success was the result of highly concessionary terms to industry and based on probably one of the largest and richest resource bases of copper and gold in the world, and the largest in Asia at the time. Instead of looking directly at the CoW, this issue may be better analyzed by more general comparison with successful mining regulatory regimes and investment regimes. The most successful regulatory regimes link exploration rights to the right to mine and do not restrict profits past a quantifiable return to the government.

Pros: The form of contract allows the government to be seen by constituents as active in projects when from a capacity standpoint it is not able to be so. Model terms or standardized forms are generally used. The investor has sufficient confidence in the contract over time and in the quantifiable returns to justify a level of investment that would not be justified in mere 'service contracts'.

Cons: A model hybrid contract needs to be very carefully drafted or the amount of government control will not provide sufficient investor confidence in the stability of the contract. Also, constituent and community expectations of the relationship (that they 'own' the project) do not often match reality and can lead to problems.

Joint ventures - Two entities jointly agree to operate a business to undertake a project (such as mineral exploration, development and production). An example in the Asia-Pacific region is China's joint venture law that mandates a certain percentage of domestic ownership of the joint venture. Usually a joint venture is governed by an operating agreement for a domestically registered company that determines responsibilities, capital and other contributions, and which parties assume which risks. In the minerals sector, a joint venture can either integrate the

concession agreement within its operating agreements (if the government and a private investor are the parties to the agreement), or two companies (for example, a domestic company and an international investor) who form a joint venture can then enter into a concession agreement with the government (for example, Lane Xang Minerals in Lao PDR).

Pros: Agreements are very flexible and can be tailored to specific projects and the respective companies' duties, authority and responsibilities. The agreements can be crafted in many ways and have a long successful track record in many industries and sectors.

Cons: The assumption of risk for a successful project is a significant issue especially in the minerals sector. Most more mature regulatory agencies have learned that revenue is generated earlier and is maximized through royalty and taxation rather than with a percentage of equity in a company, although transitional and developing governments rarely accept this concept, wanting to directly have a share in the profits. There is also significant conflict of interest between the government as an economic actor and as a regulator. Liability is also an issue as a government can waive its sovereign immunity when it acts for economic gain under international law.

Production Sharing Agreements - Generally utilized where a State-run company (e.g. a petroleum company) enters into an agreement with an investor company to develop and produce a resource and then splits or shares the actual production between them in a defined manner. It generally follows a systematic agreement to split the production into three parts: one that will pay production costs; one belonging to the company; and one belonging to the government. Because of the physical differences between oil and gas and hard rock minerals (relating to the recovery, transportation, distribution, sale and use of the commodity), most countries do not use production sharing for minerals. The exceptions are where transportation and processing are relatively straightforward, such as in the Central Asian Republics and where the commodity is used as a means to develop domestic industry. The Philippines, for example, has used production-sharing contracts for mining for domestic companies.

Pros: The government is seen to 'own' a percentage of the recovered minerals. Politically, it tends to be more acceptable to constituents and communities than other types of agreements.

Cons: The biggest drawbacks, especially for developing countries, are:

1. A State-run minerals 'authority' such as electricity or oil and gas does not exist, or there is little capacity to deal with production sharing.

2. Profit margins for oil and gas are generally much higher (70 to 80 per cent) so there is more revenue to split and the agreement to split is easier to reach.

3. Countries can directly use oil and gas, but not minerals.

4. Common accounting principles have been developed for petroleum, but not for minerals. Classes of costs, treatment of overheads other matters regarding the management of transfer pricing risk are often absent in mineral legislation.

5. As in field decommissioning and funds for closure-rehabilitation, restoration and closure are not as standardized for minerals, and entail much more work and variability.

6. Price volatility in minerals is greater.

7. Exploration, development and production for minerals is much more difficult and hard to know at exploration stage.

8. Negotiation for production-sharing contracts (PSC) for minerals is very difficult and time-consuming (usually requiring a different technical set of skills for negotiators) and contracts must be carefully structured; because of the uncertainties companies will often require more leeway.

Specialty and other agreements - Examples include tax stabilization agreements where a company might agree to pay a higher percentage in order to receive an assurance that the fiscal terms surrounding a concession agreement will not change. Specific 'phase of life-cycle' agreements, such as processing agreements, marketing agreements or off-take agreements are also common. The issue for developing country governments is often whether they will be a party to such agreements and whether they will earn revenue from these contracts. In addition, sub-contracts for specific parts of an operation are common and have similar issues, especially where there is less capacity to capture income taxes for trans-border contracts.

Model Contracts - The Model Mineral Development Agreement (MMDA) Version 1 (MMDA, 2011) - one of the two main model contracts developed recently - is a concession-type agreement. This project was undertaken by the International Bar Association's Mining Committee to provide both governments and companies a model agreement that incorporates an optimum balance of risks and rewards for mineral development projects. The project reviewed approximately 60 agreements and selected out 'the best' legal and subject matter clauses. The first version was circulated for comment and was reviewed by government, company and community lawyers, although the predominant participation was by academia and pro-industry groups.

Model Community Development Agreements - The World Bank has worked on a 'Model Community Development Agreement' (World Bank, 2012) that would provide fiscal and development benefits to communities affected by mine sites and provide other regional development. In the PN exploitation case, no specific mine site community exists (except perhaps for affected fauna and flora). As a result, provisions that will determine what kind of fiscal and development benefits from PN exploitation will not need to be in a separate agreement negotiated with a specific mine site community. These provisions can be included either in the PN exploitation statutory regime or within a project-specific contract.

Analysis Regarding Agreements for PN Exploitation

With regards to PN exploration, the ISA used standardized clauses for agreements that were included as an annex to the Exploration Regulations. The question with regard to PN exploitation will again be whether the ISA wants standardized provisions for a contract or whether the contracts should be partially or fully negotiable. When considering what kind of contract the ISA might want to utilize for PN exploitation, the most important *project-specific* factors are likely to be, *inter alia*:

1. Provisional or tenured licences.

2. Prefeasibility and feasibility studies, including environmental impact studies.

3. Plan of work terms and conditions:
   a. Production estimates
   b. Annual expenditures
   c. Infrastructure
   d. Transportation
   e. Downstream processing and marketing
   f. Trade considerations
   g. Environmental management and compliance plans
   h. Personnel and staffing specifics (mine manager, engineers, environmental manager, nationalities of employees)
   i. Data and specimen storage
   j. Training
   k. Other corporate social responsibility and obligations

4. Specific warranties and guarantees from individual companies, parent companies and sponsoring States.

5. Business formation, host or sponsoring country and recognized obligations thereto.

6. Revenue requirements (including fees and royalties) and stages when those returns are required - early in the project to satisfy developing country needs or will total value of return be more important?

7. Distribution of costs (for example, capitalization of exploration costs; how will development costs be handled - deductions, amortization, loss carry forward).

8. Distribution of benefit streams to others.

9. Degree of control ISA exerts over the project (for example, some transitional governments require a seat on the board of directors).

10. Host and sponsoring State issues (including business form, 'double taxation', harmonization of regulations).

11. Equity considerations, for example, for the Enterprise.

12. Relationship with the Enterprise, if any.

13. Specialized reporting and milestone requirements.

14. Relinquishment.

15. Closure and rehabilitation requirements.

16. Financing and security interest obligations.

17. Licence restrictions and other licence considerations.

18. Liability and liquidated damages.

19. International trade issues.

20. Incorporation of the plan of work as an element of the contract.

Developing the Statutory Regime for a PN Exploitation Regime

UNCLOS and AGXI provide that exploitation regulations should be comparable to land-based mining regimes. Article 17 of Annex III provides specific areas that are to be included in regulations concerning exploitation. Given these and the discussion above it is logical to consider existing offshore regimes and to provide continuity (where necessary or desired) with previously issued regulations, such as the exploration and environmental regulations. However, for the purposes of this discussion the specific deep ocean mining concerns for PN that can be foreseen shall be addressed first. These include:

1. The status of existing concessions.

2. The amount of exploration that has occurred.

3. Anticipated mining processes for PN.

4. Mining only or mining and processing.

5. Options regarding composition of a regulatory regime.

6. Life cycle of PN exploitation.

7. Whether licences are granted solely by application or otherwise (for example, auction or tender).

8. Required environmental sensitivity under UNCLOS.

Given the above, the ISA will need to develop a regulatory method, based upon foreseeable events, to ensure slow, measured development and sufficient regulatory control over a project before it advances to the stage where, if problems arise, it can no longer be clawed back, modified or terminated. One way to accomplish this is to provide for a 'provisional' mining licence that would mandate that an operator demonstrate competence in deep ocean engineering and mining and associated environmental responsibility to the ISA before receiving a 'tenured' mining licence. In addition, to ensure competence the ISA might require a 'front-loaded' or heightened threshold for technical and financial qualification of operators comparable to traditional land-based licensing. Some of these heightened considerations have been addressed in the exploration and environmental regulations but it is suggested that they are enhanced where necessary for the PN exploitation regulations by measures including, *inter alia*:

1. Binding private company, State, State joint venture or quasi-State operators as commercial actors undertaking mining operations.

    a. Clear and unambiguous responsibilities, duties and liabilities, expanding upon those found in the exploration regulations.

    b. Nature and scope of mining rights are defined, for example, 'security of tenure', which is ambiguous (does it refer to retaining a concession and / or a right to mine) (see discussion below).

    c. Depending on the type of fiscal system implemented,[4] consideration of a multilateral agreement to ensure companies, State operators, State sponsors and downstream companies uphold their responsibilities (including harmonization of national laws) *throughout the life-cycle of the mining and downstream stages to the point where: a) fiscal obligations are fixed; b) trade implications are no longer the responsibility of the ISA; and c) the ISA is otherwise not involved.*

2. Minimum competency of contractors is ensured through heightened application thresholds.

3. Provisional mining licence for pilot site.

4. Application for a provisional mining licence to include, *inter alia*:

    a. Technical, fiscal and environmental qualifications of operator.

    b. Key staff and personnel.

    c. A prefeasibility study based on

previous exploration, transportation, processing and testing data and analysis.

   d. Plans of work in the application for a provisional mining licence to include, *inter alia*:

      i. Plans for a detailed feasibility study including a pilot commercial site.

      ii. Expenditure schedules.

      iii. Production estimates for the pilot site and after.

      iv. Environmental management plans including closure and rehabilitation.

      v. Transportation specifics.

   e. Performance assurances and guarantees.

   f. Host and sponsoring government specifics.

   g. Training and corporate social responsibility.

   h. Size and area of concession.

5. Tenured mining licence to be conditional upon:

   a. Successful completion of pilot study under provisional licence.

   b. ISA approval of the feasibility study.

6. Strict reporting, reporting standards and milestone notification to ensure adherence to work plans.

7. Audits of adherence to work plans.

8. Environmental compliance monitoring and audits.

9. 'Zero-tolerance' standard for serious or continual violations or evasive behaviour resulting in suspension or termination of a licence and closure of the site(s).

10. Substantial monetary penalties or liquidated damages can be used for less serious violations and accidents.

11. Enhanced standards and procedures for accident and disaster response and reporting.

12. Enhanced mine safety and health regulations.

13. Continual and progressive update of operating, management and environmental plans to ensure experience is progressively incorporated into mining plans and operations.

14. Use of more stringent financial surety instruments throughout the mining life cycle.

15. Liability based perhaps on different legal standard (strict liability or foreseeability rather than lower negligence standards) for misfeasance, malfeasance or omission.

These represent only the most basic issues that will need to be addressed for a PN-specific regulatory regime and a few are discussed below. In addition, other issues, such as the relationship of PN mining with the status of current concessions will be addressed.

Relationship of Mining to Existing Concessions

Although the prospect of development of an exploitation regime provides the opportunity to create a fresh regulatory approach, each existing exploration licence holder has continuing rights and obligations pursuant to their exploration licence (PN Exploration Regulation 24(2)). (ISA, 2000) These rights and obligations are present until the expiration of the licence and some obligations, especially those pertaining to the environment, may linger under various legal theories after the licence expires. At the very least, the exploration licence gives a 'priority and preference' to mine in the area in which they are working, if they apply for a mining licence. It is anticipated that some explorers will be well qualified and have no problems with demonstrating fiscal, technical, environmental and social credentials sufficient to obtain a mining licence. However, some explorers may not be able to satisfy all criteria and how these explorers will be dealt with, what their options may be and how long they will have to demonstrate satisfactory credentials will be critical, as elaborated in Regulation 24, as will be the exact status of the concession. Some explorers, while qualified, will not be in a position to begin mining and it is very likely that economically viable mining will not be possible for some time. It will be important to deal with these issues objectively. This context also raises the question of whether retention licences (also known as 'maintenance licences' in some jurisdictions) should be considered by the ISA. These licences allow an explorer to retain exploration rights and obligations, subject to payment of annual lease fees if mining is not feasible, which will preclude any other applicant from obtaining the concession.

In this regard, the differences between the rights of previous exploration licence holders and new applicants should also be carefully defined in the exploitation regulations.

A related issue is the continuation of exploration while mining is progressing at a pilot site or commercial production has begun in one part of the concession. It is very common for companies to run simultaneous exploration and mining operations in one concession. Indeed, as increased data and information come in from the mining operation, operators know better how to focus exploration and techniques for exploration become more sophisticated. As a result, questions remain about under which conditions exploration can continue in a mining concession and how will those exploration rights mesh with mining rights in terms of, *inter alia*, length of term, relinquishment, payment of lease fees for the area (whether paying at exploration or mining rates).

Security of Tenure

Security of tenure appears in Article 153, paragraph 6 of UNCLOS and in Regulation 24 of the Regulations on Prospecting and Exploration for Polymetallic Nodules in the Area (ISA, 2000). Security of tenure *as provided by contract* is not defined in the Convention.

Does the security of tenure relate only to the duration of the exploration contract or beyond? Regulation 24 provides that a contractor that has "an approved plan of work for exploration only shall have a preference and a priority among applicants submitting plans of work for exploitation of the same area and resources" and provides for dispute resolution if the preference or priority is withdrawn. Such language is ambiguous in terms of traditional mining terminology, which tends to equate security of tenure with a right to mine. These issues will need to be addressed in the exploitation regulations for decisions that the ISA will make on applications for exploitation licences regarding issues including adequacy of qualifications, adequacy of prefeasibility studies, approvals of feasibility studies.

Administrative and Lease Fees

Administrative and leasing fees will be a part of the revenue that the Authority will generate as part of the licensing process. The ISA, like every country with a resource sector, faces the issue of what kind of fees to apply, and how application, licence and land lease fees should be determined. The more mature regulatory regimes generally base their administrative fee structure on several factors, the most important of which is cost recovery to provide revenue to support regulatory and administrative activities ('user pays'). Budgetary analyses are undertaken to provide a certain percentage of the budget through fees and rents. The major types of fees and rents that are common internationally include application and permit fees, schedules of fees for services (such as review of applications), annual licence fees, and lease rents (known by names including 'surface rental') usually based on a block or area (for example, km^2, hectares). Most countries, even the more mature regulatory regimes, have struggled to reconcile the need to promote mining and keeping fee and lease rents low enough to accomplish this with charging enough to cover real administrative costs. The optimum solution appears to be to gear the fees and lease structure at the highest amount, such that they do not unduly discourage mining or negatively affect project profitability while attempting to recover costs to ease the burden on taxpayers, or in the current situation, the member States.

It should be noted that most mature regulatory regimes do not attempt to simply increase revenue through fees and lease rents, as this can deter legitimate investment. It is economically more efficient and palatable to industry to accomplish revenue generation through royalty and taxation.

Another consideration is that if there is no attempt to move towards a 'user pays' system to pay for the administration of the regime, all of the member States will essentially be subsidizing the administration of the regulatory regime, which over time becomes a political issue if some countries are perceived as benefitting more than others from deep-sea resource exploitation The ISA may wish to undertake cost/benefit studies to assist in the determination of optimum levels of fees and rents.

The theory that certain levels of fees and rents discourage speculation has governed the way they have been imposed. Given, however, the staged licensing scheme and application requirements (including pre-feasibility and full feasibility studies) that are recommended herein, this may be of less concern at the PN exploitation stage. This concern is also related to the question of allowing retention licences (and their respective fees and lease rents), and how long the ISA will allow exploration licence holders to hold their concessions without applying for an exploitation licence. A related issue is that some countries, for example, India, collect 'dead rents' that are generally scaled to the time the licence is held for concessions that are not being worked. Generally, however, the imposition of fees and rents to reduce speculation should not be an alternative to proactive regulatory oversight to ensure that companies are adhering to plans of work and moving along the continuum from exploration to mining.

The Commonwealth of Australia's Offshore Minerals Act of 1994 and subsidiary legislation (Table 1) provides an example of current fees applicable to offshore mineral concessions. The 1994 Act does not provide for annual lease fees outside of licence fees. Another issue requiring consideration is the reservation of authority to adjust, change or add fees and lease rents. In addition, there must be consideration of the methods used to justify those changes as either one-off or periodic (for example, reference to indexes such as cost of living).

Table 1: Australia's Offshore Minerals Act and subsidiary legislation provisions

Commonwealth of Australia (offshore minerals)	Application fee: AUD 3,000	Mining Licence Fee: AUD 200/block	Registration Fee: Percentage of value of licence, share or interest 1.5%
	Works Licence fee: AUD 20/hectare of works area	Works Licence fee: AUD 20/hectare	Other registration and administrative fees between AUD 600-3,000
	Retention Licence fee: AUD 3,000	Retention Licence fee: AUD 200/block	

Types of Fees and Lease Rents

There are almost as many types of application fees, annual fees and lease rents as there are countries and regulatory agencies. The following list provides an overview of the various types that can be considered:

1. Application fee for grant of mineral development licence.
2. Application fee for renewal of mineral development licence.
3. Application fee to record agreement.
4. Application fee to consolidate mining leases.
5. Application fee for amendment of relinquishment condition.
6. Application fee for grant or renewal of mining lease.
7. Application fee for non-competitive lease application.
8. Application fee for competitive lease application.
9. Fee (one-time or annual) mineral development licence.
10. Fee for recording mining licence.
11. Fee for mining licence registration.
12. Fee for advertisement.
13. Fee (one-time or annual) for mining lease.
14. Fee (one-time or annual) for tailings disposal permit.
15. Fee (one-time or annual) for waste disposal.
16. Fee to sublease mining lease.
17. Fee to transfer mineral development licence.
18. Fee to transfer mining lease.
19. Lodging fees for documents at registrar (for example, notice of surrender, revised plans of work).
20. Fee to assign licence or lease.
21. Fees to obtain copies.
22. Fees for request to record changes.
23. Fees for late submission.
24. Fees for search and extract.
25. Data acquisition fees.
26. Fee for greenhouse gas permit.
27. Fee for water monitoring.
28. Fee for conduct of inspection.
29. Fees for laboratory and sample preparation and analysis.
30. Fee for notice of protest.

While past exploration for deep-sea resources has largely been undertaken by States or State-sponsored companies, it is anticipated that private or State-sponsored companies may wish to undertake mining projects in the future. Most mining by private companies is undertaken with borrowed money, with the licence being an important security interest (for example, whether pledged, mortgaged) for the funding. For a deep-sea mining licence, security interests will be a difficult issue likely to complicate international financing.

A related issue is that it is normal practice in mature mining regimes for mining licences to be easily conveyed or transferred to successor companies. While it is important to allow for conveyance or transfer, because of the heightened sensitivity to technical difficulty and environmental concerns, the regulations will necessarily be similar to the exploration regulations, which require that any successor be able to demonstrate the ability to undertake the project and be subject to ISA approval. These requirements may make deep-sea PN exploitation projects significantly less desirable because they incorporate more risk to the operators by further breaking the chain of the right to mine. However, operators will need to recognize that the ISA mandate to avoid and mitigate environmental damage will require such terms and conditions. It is therefore in the best interests of both mining companies and the ISA to ensure that training and development of mining technology progress in all haste.

Companies may also wish to sublease, farming out specific parts of the operation, such as transportation or processing. It will be important that contractors are specifically responsible and liable for all sublet or subcontracted operations. Subleases and subcontractors should also be required to provide performance guarantees to the ISA where appropriate.

Safeguarding Resources

A topic of increasing international interest is 'safeguarding' resources. This refers to the governance and management of resources to ensure that other activities do not impinge or spoil known resources, and also to the issue of ensuring that a resource is exploited to the optimal degree. Some issues regarding safeguarding are not present in the deep-sea context, such as not allowing other development to hinder or spoil a known resource, but others are relevant to the ISA in the 'optimal exploitation' sense. In land-based mining, 'high-grading' is a serious problem facing regulators. It occurs when an operator mines only the best grade of resource and leaves or spoils the rest of the lower grade resource. It can also refer to the degree of processing that an operator pursues for a specific type of ore and how much and how many associated minerals are recovered. The ISA can anticipate that there will be keen interest in how it will oversee and 'safeguard' deep-sea PN resources.

Meshing the Environmental Regulations for Exploration with the Mining Code

As mining operations in the deep-sea progress to development and actual mining on a scale larger than that allowed in the exploration phase, the ongoing activities of the ISA, with respect to environmental management of exploration and potential exploitation (ISA, 2011), will need to be reviewed to ensure they are sufficient in the context of the exploitation regime. There will be a need for ISA to develop a separate set of environmental regulations governing mining. As part of the application process, a company should be required to submit a report analyzing the environmental aspects of its exploration operations. Based on that data, information and analysis, a prefeasibility study should be required as part of the application for a provisional mining

licence. A key part of the prefeasibility study would include an environmental impact statement and a proposed environmental management plan (EMP). Insufficient data for this level of reporting, analysis and input into a prefeasibility study means that the operator has not gathered enough information to proceed with provisional mining.

Grant of Concessions via Auction

Many concessions of unprecedented size have been granted for prospective PN areas. A stepped and conditional licensing procedure similar to that discussed above can be developed for those concessions where exploration has taken place and the explorers wish to apply for a provisional mining licence. For areas where an exploration licence was granted but where, for example, the operator is not qualified and the preference is withdrawn by the ISA, or the operator chooses not to go forward to the mining stage, the ISA may want to consider an auction or bidding system, similar to that used for oil and gas. While mineral development is generally less suited to an auction situation than petroleum, this solution may merit discussion.

Tenders for Mineral Concessions by Highest Qualified Bid

The international oil and gas sector has utilized tenders for concessions for many years. This is largely because the technology for the development of oil and gas, although dependent on the area in which it takes place, is well known and relatively standardized, with many companies actively vying for concessions. However, tenders via bidding procedures for mineral projects have been less often utilized by governments, largely because of the unique risks, costs and development concerns inherent in mining projects. Bidding procedures have been most used where countries have tendered known geologically prospective areas to companies. In the case of PN, geological prospectivity is relatively well known.

There are definite issues, both for and against, involved in utilizing bidding procedures for prospective mineral properties. For areas that might be competitively tendered, the following issues will be relevant to both companies and State-sponsored companies:

1. Is there sufficient geological information available for the concession area to be analyzed by a company to determine the amount of the resource and economic potential on which to base a bid?

2. Will there be sufficient geological information available for the concession area for the ISA to place an 'upset', 'reserve' or 'minimum' price or is the ISA willing to tender an area without one or to commission an independent valuation?

3. Is there sufficient interest by companies in a sufficient number of areas to justify putting in place:

   a. A bidding procedure through legislation, and to

   b. Marshal the necessary administrative resources to do so?

4. Has there been a detailed cost/benefit study prepared to determine that revenue to the government will be greater through a bidding arrangement than by utilizing more accepted and recognized leasing and licensing arrangements?

5. What will be the basis of the bid for the concession?

   a. 'Bonus bidding'.

   b. Cost of work programme.

   c. Total anticipated investment?

6. What will happen after the bids are analyzed and a winner is awarded the concession?

7. Will a contract be negotiated? Will the contract terms be affected by the amount of the bid?

8. How will environmental management and corporate social responsibility be included in the bidding system?

9. What type of auction may be appropriate? Different types include 'lottery', open or sealed bids.

Major issues of concern with respect to tenders are given in Table 2. It should also be noted that aside from oil and gas, many countries have utilized tenders for bids for mineral properties in the past with varying levels of success. Some recent examples are presented in Table 3.

Table 2: Issues concerning tenders for mineral concessions

Issue	Relevant Inquiry
Level of interest by companies	Is there sufficient interest by companies to justify bid process?
	Would the 'right' kind of companies be interested in bidding for these auctions, for example companies with proven technical, social and environmental track records? How many companies or States would need to express interest? How would interest be expressed to trigger a tender?
Cost/benefit analysis of tenders	Is this kind of process of more or less benefit to the ISA (as opposed to mining licences)? Tender fees can provide additional revenue but there are issues with respect to how tender fees will be handled.
Bidding structure	One- or two-tier structure (technical and/or competitive)
Pre-qualification of bidders	How would bidders be pre-qualified?
	Would there be minimum experience and work programme thresholds for Companies? How would these be determined? Who would determine these?
Pre-tender meetings and site visit	Compulsory or not? What site-specific knowledge would be required for PN?
Bid review and selection	How would the ISA correlate programme quality and monetary bid amount (assuming that a better quality work programme and operations would cost more than a poorer quality programme and operations)?
	How would the ISA compare bids from disparately qualified companies?
	Does the ISA have the necessary expertise and competence to accurately judge company qualifications, experience and work programmes to obtain the best-qualified and highest-monetary bid (again, most developing countries with limited staff and staff experience find this aspect of tendering areas extremely difficult)?
	Can ISA decisions on the above be quantified in order to justify selection of certain companies in a transparent and open manner?
	Would the tender process be included in the mining law or other law?
	Can this kind of auction be compromised by bidding collusion? By corruption? What realistic and concrete safeguards can be put into place to reduce these risks?
Undertaking cost	What kind of financial assurances would be required to assure performance?
Grounds for bid termination?	What would be grounds for termination?

Table 3:   Examples of mineral tenders

Country	Bidding Process	Comments
China	Exploration and Mining Rights, Tender, Auction and Bidding Management Tentative Procedures, MOLAR, 11 June 2003, eff. 1 August 2003.	Where there are areas where exploration (with sufficient information to support finding of viable asset) or mining rights have expired, or where the State has funded exploration, the State or province level MOLAR can determine that an auction, tender or bid is appropriate. Foreign mining companies can follow incorporation laws to participate (although significant uncertainty exists in procedures) *Auction* - there must be a minimum of three bidders; winning bid must be higher than reserve price set by government (valuation can be commissioned by province or State bureau); *Tender* - notice posted 60 to 90 days in advance; each participant will file a tender package. Proposal minimum of 3 tenders; Bidding - for mining rights, public notice must be posted 20 days in advance; bid period runs for 10 days; highest bid will be posted at venue of bid (replaced by higher bids as received); at end of 10-day period, highest bid is accepted; None of the above used for extensions, renewal. After award, a contract must be signed with State Example: in Xinjiang in 2004, 7 mines auctioned for 22 million USD
Ukraine		Privatization of iron ore mine and steel production plant; has been controversial with largest bid not being accepted in favour of smaller bid by domestic consortium
France	French Mining Code, amended 1994; "*mise en concurrence*"	Based on explicit technical and financial qualifications
Tanzania	Tanzanian Mining Act	Utilizes an alternative tender system when Minister determines that public interest is best served by invitation of applications for tender; review of bids includes proposed work programme, expenditure commitments, financial and technical resources, previous experience of applicant in exploration and mining

Country	Bidding Process	Comments
Peru	Private Investment Promotion Agency auctions mineral properties	Example, in 2004 Xstrata acquired Las Bambas (30,000 ha of land) through auction; $121 million US bid provides for upfront payment of $91 million for option right and US $30 million during option and construction phases; base price for bidding was US $40 million plus 2% royalty; company will have 6 years to complete exploration and feasibility work; social development fund to get $21 million over life cycle of mine if option is exercised
Indonesia	New Law on Mineral and Coal Mining ('Minerba'), 16 Dec.2008 (not yet effective).	Minerals can be subject to auction for exploration through feasibility ('IUP') and production ('IUPK') similar to oil and gas; however, the law has not been signed and regulations governing the procedure have not been issued
Nigeria	Bureau for Public Enterprises runs tenders for deregulation of coal and mining sectors	Initial auction for privatized assets was unsuccessful due to low turnout of bidders; applicants must be pre-qualified and pay a nominal fee (approx. US $200) per mining area for bid documents; of 13 developed mining areas, only 6 initially auctioned
United States	1920 Mineral Leasing Act for 'KMAs' (known mineral areas) Bureau of Land Management (BLM) Energy and Minerals Division; mostly oil and gas	System has evolved through several types of competitive bidding including lotteries, open, oral, sealed and minimum acceptable bidding procedures.

The common parameters of successful tenders appear to be:

1. Relatively clear understanding of geology and distribution of anticipated resources, that is, more mature areas of development rather than properties that require significantly more exploration to define resource areas.

2. Companies are familiar and comfortable with the tender and bid process.

3. Bidding process is open, transparent and subject to question via dispute resolution to counter possible fraud, collusion and corruption in the tender process.

4. The process after the tender is well understood (for example, negotiation of an investment contract).

If the ISA is interested in further investigation of the possibility of auctioning PN exploitation blocks the following issues will be important:

1. Issuance of Notice of Auction.

2. Instructions to Bidders.

3. Required submissions of bidders including:
   a. Pre-feasibility study.
   b. Technical, financial and corporate social responsibility pre-qualification.
   c. Plan of work.
   d. Criteria for selection.

4. Issuance of provisional licence conditional upon completion and approval of feasibility study.

Other Considerations for Licensing PN Exploitation

Additional provisions and issues for consideration in developing PN exploitation regulations include:

1. Mining Licence.
   a. Criteria for issuance:
      i. Priority.
      ii. First in time.
      iii. Tender.
   b. Time for consideration.
   c. Form of issuance.
   d. Term.
   e. Conditions.
   f. Amendments.
   g. Renewal.
   h. Suspension.
   i. Termination.
   j. Retention licence.
   k. Restrictions (for example other activities such as fishing).
2. Mining lease (basis for lease rents).
3. Contract.
4. Location of concession.
5. Rights and duties:
   a. Security of tenure.
   b. Access to concession and resources.
   c. Assurance of performance:
      i. Types of security.
      ii. Form of security.
      iii. Calculations of security.
      iv. Forfeiture of security.
   d. Corporate social responsibility including training.
6. Plan of work.
7. Pre-feasibility studies (discussed in separate section below).
8. Feasibility studies.
9. Reporting:
   a. Required reports.
   b. Form or reports.
10. Data and sample retention.
11. Research:
   a. Operator scientific and technical research.
   b. Third party scientific and technical research.
   c. Observers.
12. Exploration.
13. Labour.
14. Accidents:
   a. Immediate reporting.
   b. Response.
15. Mining safety and health (for example equipment requirements):
   a. Inspections.
   b. Power to inspect.
   c. Access to concession by inspectors.
   d. Routine inspections.
   e. Spot inspections.
16. Reports:
   a. Violations.
   b. Notice of violation.
   c. Time to remedy.
   d. Required response to violation.
   e. Cease and desist orders.
17. Infrastructure development and removal.
18. Transportation and shipping:
   a. Delivery of ore to port.
   b. Delivery of ore for smelting.
19. Relationship of contractor with Enterprise.
20. Gazetting of licences and concessions.
21. Dispute Resolution.
22. Force majeure regulation of other activities.
23. Regulation and other activities.
24. Offences:
   a. Warnings.
   b. Offense notification.
   c. Theft of minerals – removal, concealment, spoliation, wasted.
   d. Fraud, misrepresentation and omission.
   e. Obstruction of inspectors.
   f. Obstruction of third parties, e.g. third party obstruction.
   g. Penalties.
   h. Penalty notification.
25. Host and sponsoring State issues.

Capacity of the ISA to Negotiate, Administrate, Oversee, Monitor, Inspect and Enforce Regulations

Although it is not the purpose of this paper to discuss the organization or administrative structure of the ISA, it is critical to note that land-based mineral exploration, development and exploitation activities are normally set forth in specific national mineral policy and legislation - in a similar way to the present activities being undertaken by the ISA for the Area. However, on land the actual implementation, administration, oversight, inspection and compliance assurance activities associated with mineral exploitation are almost always carried out by a specific responsible agency, such as a Ministry or Bureau, whose role is also defined in the abovementioned policy and legislation.

Such a responsible agency does not presently exist within the ISA, which in accordance with the evolutionary approach to its establishment reflected in the 1994 Agreement, has been principally acting as an international organization providing meeting services to member States and expert bodies. However, the present high level of interest, coupled with the need of many operators to apply for exploitation licences by 2016, means that detailed discussions for the funding, planning and implementation of such an 'administrative agency' capacity within the ISA are crucial in the near future. It is recommended that the ISA undertake a comparative analysis of representative 'administrative agencies' as a basis for the development of a similar capacity within the Authority. This capacity would need to include transparent funding mechanisms, on a cost-recovery or alternative basis, secure data management and analysis, maintenance of a mining claims registry to international standards (ISO 4001) and financial and accounting capacity.

PN Exploitation Regulations: Formulating the Regulations to be Part of the Whole

Although this discussion focuses on considerations for developing a framework for PN exploitation regulations, due consideration should be paid to the role these regulations will play in the overall regulatory regime. The structure and substance of the regulatory regime for PN are the same as those necessary for the regulation of exploitation of other deep-sea resources. While PN nodules are the subject of the current enquiry, this is because they are the first resource that may be exploited (or at least the first being considered for exploitation), and not because they should be regulated in a different manner. Indeed, it is advisable to consider the ISA regime for PN exploitation as a template for future regulation of mineral exploitation to the extent that ultimately, the exploitation regulations should be unified in some manner.

International Trade Issues

Pursuant to AGXI Section 6, 'Production Policy', production shall be in accordance with the General Agreement on Trade and Tariffs (GATT), and allow neither subsidies, discrimination by source nor preferential access to markets, with limited exceptions. Given the recent WTO decisions against China concerning impermissible export restrictions on raw materials (WTO, 2012) and the fact that China is being considered as a processor for PN, it is anticipated that the international trade implications of PN exploitation will require careful consideration by the ISA. In addition, many other developing countries that have or wish to develop processing capabilities have included export restrictions in their respective legislation or policy within recent years (for example, Indonesia, Vietnam).

Section 6, article 6 of AGXI provides that the ISA "shall develop rules, regulations and procedures which ensure the implementation of the provisions of this section, including relevant rules, regulations and procedures governing the approval of plans of work." In addition to developing these rules, regulations and procedures, and by providing that plans of work include safeguards against impermissible trade practices (for example specification of processing agreements, off-take agreements, specification and use of ports, and ship and vessel registries), the use of multilateral agreements to bind State Parties could also be considered to discourage impermissible trade practices.

Conclusion

The ISA's choice and mix of legal components for the regulatory regime will require careful harmonization to address the deep sea exploitation of PN, achieve its UNCLOS-mandated results and avoid the pitfalls that plague many governments regulating land-based mining. Each selected component should provide clarity and transparency, and ensure the most secure tenure possible for qualified investors. Analysis of the components should be undertaken to understand how they will affect investment decisions and ensure that only qualified investors are able to operate. Lastly, each of the components and their implementation should reflect the Authority's mandate to exploit the common heritage of mankind for the benefit of mankind as a whole, and be an unquestioned example of good governance.

Notes

1. 'Operator', 'contractor' and 'company' will be used interchangeably in this Section.

2. For example, companies are unintentionally encouraged to 'high-grade' through a poorly conceived or constructed fiscal regime, resulting in lower grade resources that are either left undeveloped or spoiled from ever being developed.

3. The terms 'contract' and 'agreement' are used interchangeably within this discussion although technically contracts (which are susceptible to legal enforcement) in some jurisdictions are a subset of agreements. The actual form, if not the name, of the final agreement will need be standardized for enforceability pursuant to the applicable law under which it will be reviewed and interpreted.

4. There has been some discussion regarding ore 'free on board' (FOB) being the last point of ISA authority and responsibility, although this will only be possible if a royalty or other measure is implemented based solely on tonnage and grade, and with sufficient monitoring to assure the ISA of accurate reporting.

4. Use of Feasibility Studies in the Regulation of Deep Ocean Polymetallic Nodule Exploitation

Overview

For deep ocean PN exploitation to become a reality, a sound regulatory regime is required that provides for the objective assessment of a project from geological, technical, economic, financial, environmental and social standpoints prior to the issuance of a mining licence. In the PN exploitation context, a feasibility study <u>will be the process and provide the benchmarks</u> by which a company demonstrates to the ISA, host or sponsoring countries, financiers, possible partners and others that all relevant challenges surrounding a deep ocean mining project can be overcome to develop a safe, viable and profitable mining project with sufficient revenue to contribute to the development of the common heritage of mankind.

There are two key components to the feasibility studies in the staged scenario discussed in this report. The first is a formal 'pre-feasibility report' that will be required to obtain a provisional mining licence to undertake a pilot project. Governments generally do not require a formal pre-feasibility study report to be submitted and they are most often used by the company to determine, based on all the data and information it has gathered and the analyses it has undertaken, whether to pursue a project after exploration. A critical point here is that during the latter part of the exploration phase, site testing and processing tests are allowed, which tend to generate more than normal exploration results compared to land-based exploration. However, in July 2012, Secretary-General Odunton noted (ISA, 2012) that "no contractor holding a licence to explore for these minerals had notified the Authority on its intention to undertake such tests which would determine the level of commercial viability." Nor has an integrated

mining system, even on a pilot scale, been demonstrated. As a result, from a regulatory standpoint, it cannot be presumed that this capability currently exists.

After exploration, a company generally undertakes a pre-feasibility study to determine, according to its own in-house criteria, whether there is a sufficient resource and whether favorable conditions exist to justify commissioning a full feasibility study to be used to seek funding and government approval for a mining licence. The pre-feasibility study also provides an analytical method for the company to define the optimum parameters of the project to continue to the full feasibility stage. However, because of the frontier aspect of deep ocean mining and engineering and the associated environmental sensitivities, this 'provisional mining licence' stage has been recommended to ensure a real demonstration of mining and environmental competence prior to a grant of a full tenured licence.

This is not likely be met enthusiastically by industry or States interested in mining. However, as is recognized by all involved, deep ocean mining is faced with a 'Catch-22' situation, whereby competence can not be gained without actual mining at a commercial scale, but at the same time mining should not be allowed without prior demonstration of competence. Hence, this intermediate approach has been recommended, which requires a provisional mining licence based upon a prefeasibility study. Based upon success of the pilot mining project and the critical data and information that will be obtained from it, a full feasibility study can then be undertaken and included in an application for a tenured mining licence.

Factors that will be important in considering the parameters of the provisional mining licence, pre- feasibility study and pilot project phase will include, *inter alia*:

1. Determining an appropriate scale and term of a pilot project that will be relevant and meaningful in terms of providing adequate input for the full feasibility study and for ISA to make licensing decisions. Possibilities include:

    a. Scaled to resource (for example, a chosen tonnage or percentage, being careful not to skew reporting or decisions based upon strategic or competitive long-term licensing and recovery strategies).

    b. Time of licence (for example, six months, one year, geared to seasons).

    c. Combination (for example, x recovery or one year, whichever is earliest).

2. Provide sufficient return of resource and revenue to justify the pilot project.

3. Consider whether a different treatment of fiscal terms should be allowed during the pilot project in order to offset its short-term nature (in case it is not successful)?

4. Timeframe under which a pre-feasibility study may be undertaken and consequences of failure to comply prior to expiration of licence.

Pre-feasibility Study

Based upon the approach outlined above, a pre-feasibility study could be required along with a plan of work for an application for a provisional mining licence. It would be a study based on the site-specific geological, technical, economic, financial and environmental data and information gathered during the PN exploration phases. It would have to be in a form and contain substance sufficient to justify the grant of a provisional licence by the ISA, backed up by analysis of: a) what information can a company realistically generate for a pre-feasibility study at the end of the exploration stage for deep-ocean PN; and b) whether that information as analyzed in a feasibility study will provide the ISA sufficient basis (along with the application and plan of work) to approve a provisional mining licence.

The ISA would need to determine whether - based on a) and b) above - the status of existing data and information from the exploration stages analyzed and presented in a feasibility study (which in this approach includes an environmental impact statement) would provide sufficient information for a licensing decision to be made. A provisional mining licence approach would also allow the ISA to ramp up its oversight and inspection functions for projects that are less than full multi-decade mining projects.

A pre-feasibility study would therefore have to include an analysis and presentation of existing data and information materially affecting the outcome of the project. The major elements of a pre-feasibility study that would provide the ISA with the information needed to make a licensing decision include:

1. Selection and rationale for pilot mining area:

    a. Representative of larger resource.

    b. Commercial scale.

    c. Geographic conditions.

    d. Engineering conditions.

    e. Nearest ports, sourcing ports and processing destination.

2. Geology and resource - target reserves and resource for the pilot project:

    a. Distribution, sizes of nodules and grades according to recognized international reserve and resource classifications.

    b. Geologic models.

    c. Confidence levels, quality assurance and control.

3. Proposed mining method(s), design and mine models:

    a. Justification and optimization.

    b. Anticipated challenges.

    c. Must be commercial scale.

4. Tailings and waste disposal.

5. Other proposed surface, subsurface and

seabed infrastructure.

6. Transportation.

7. Full environmental impact assessment.

8. Project economics including cash flow analysis based on mine models:

   a. Production estimates.

   b. Capital, development and operations costs.

   c. Recovery costs.

   d. Tailings disposal costs.

   e. Processing costs.

   f. Environmental management costs (including further baseline studies).

   g. Downstream processes (marketing, sales) and costs.

   h. Revenue to ISA.

   i. Fees and other fiscal requirements on the project .

   j. Accounting methods and standards.

   k. Sourcing and access to resources needed for mine operations.

   l. Other material factors, inputs and assumptions.

9. Financing:

   a. Terms.

   b. Conditions (such as security interests).

   c. Restrictions.

10. Proposed training and social corporate governance.

11. Further exploration during pilot project.

12. Host and sponsoring state support.

13. Risk assessment and mitigation.

14. Verification or certification of key components.

15. Warranties of the accuracy of data and information from preparers and company officials.

Each of these elements requires further elaboration, which is unfortunately outside the scope of this discussion. Based on these and other elements deemed appropriate, the company, the host and sponsoring states,

financiers and the ISA will be able to review material factors of the project (based upon existing data, information and analysis of exploration data) to determine the safety and economic viability of a pilot project.

Assuming that the pilot project proceeds under a provisional licence and approaches the end of its term, the next considerations will be:

1. Data, reporting and analysis required at the end of the pilot project.

2. Factors to determine a successful pilot project:

   a. Obligations fulfilled.

   b. Mining processes successfully demonstrated.

   c. Verification of avoidance or acceptable minimal impact on environment.

   d. Production estimates verified.

   e. Refinement of resource estimations.

   f. Relinquishment.

3. Result of an unsuccessful pilot project

   a. Withdrawal of preference.

   b. Opportunity to cure.

   c. Dispute resolution.

   d. Relinquishment.

   e. Rehabilitation.

   f. Termination.

4. What constitutes approval of the pilot project from the ISA (for example, letter, certification).

5. Commencement of full feasibility study.

6. Time to undertake full feasibility study.

7. Elements of a full feasibility study (discussed below).

8. Approval of the feasibility study.

9. When may the company apply for a tenured licence.

Feasibility Study

After successful completion of a pilot project, and consistent with most land-based mining regulatory regimes, an approved full feasibility study including an updated environmental impact study will be required. This kind of feasibility study is also known as a 'bankable feasibility study' as it includes confidence levels of reserves and resources and cost estimates that are sufficiently precise for a bank to determine whether to lend money for the project (Nethery, 2003). Internationally, the most developed countries have developed systems, standards and certifications, for example the Joint Ore Reserves Committee standards, for reporting at the feasibility study stage and for public offerings via a stock market (for example, Canada, Australia, United Kingdom, United States).

These standards have been developed over a course of centuries of hard earned experience with the vagaries of exploration and mining company estimations and economic reporting. While they will expect to comply with such standards, developing country companies and States often do not require or recognize these levels of reporting, so the ISA may

need to require third-party verification and certification, at a minimum, for reserve and resource estimates and key components of a feasibility study. To begin the feasibility study process, a company should be required to submit:

1. A notification that a full feasibility study will commence.

2. The party undertaking the feasibility study or providing certification.

3. Quality assurance and control.

4. An estimated budget for the feasibility study.

5. Time frame for completing a feasibility study.

For a general context of confidence levels of data, information and analysis at various points along the life cycle of exploration and development of a mine see Figure 2.

Figure 2:   Expected Accuracy of Cost Estimates

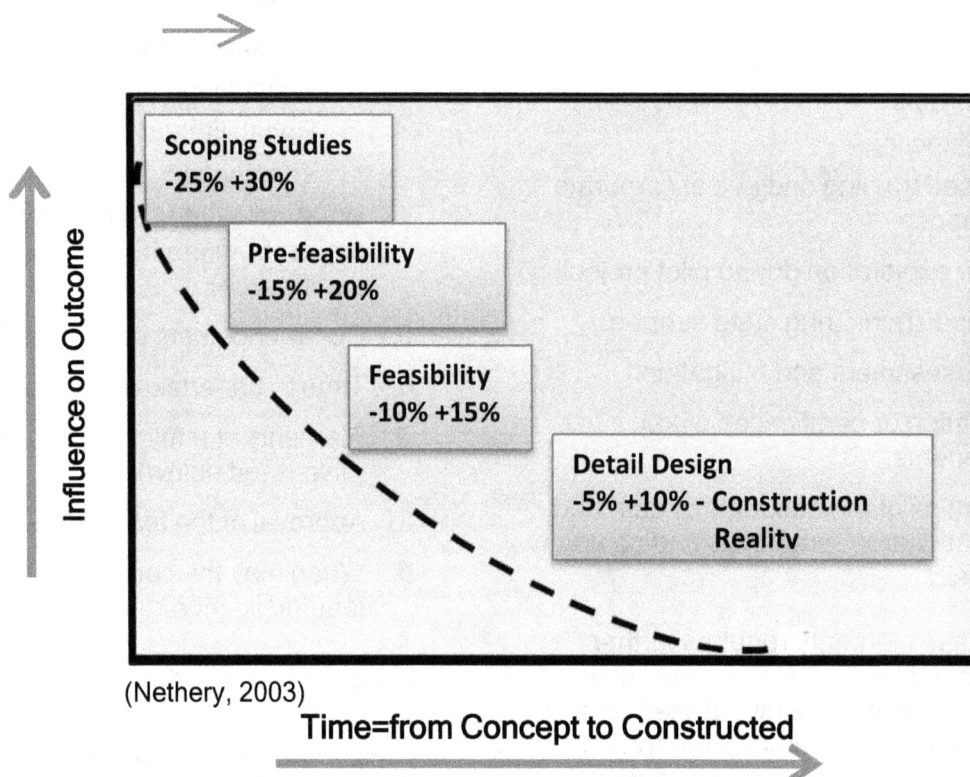

(Nethery, 2003)

Time=from Concept to Constructed

Most land-based mining regimes provide for a time frame of one to two years to complete a feasibility study, although that time often includes test mining and test processing. As a result, it is anticipated that in the context of PN exploitation a feasibility study should take no more than two years, as it should entail primarily the analysis of data and information from the pilot project and its extension to full commercial scale.

Other considerations for a full feasibility study in addition to those elements required for the pre-feasibility study that are specific to PN exploitation include:

1. Location/area:
   a. Coordinates.
   b. Relinquishment.
   c. Further exploration - retention licences.
2. Preparation of full feasibility study: the company, an independent third-party and/or an independent and certified third-party must verify key assumptions and results (including reserves and resources, environmental baselines and analysis).
3. Full environmental impact assessment and management and monitoring plans incorporating pilot project results.
4. Full economic and financial analysis including cash flow analysis from a tailored mine model and annual production estimates.
5. Mining processes, designs and plans as refined from the pilot project.
6. Metallurgy and processing as refined from the pilot project.
7. International marketing analysis and plans.
8. Anticipated trade implications.

9. Compliance with international and national laws.
10. Host country and sponsoring country requirements and implications.
11. Sourcing plans and access to resources for mine operations.
12. Labour and staffing plans.
13. Mine safety and health.
14. Corporate social responsibility.
15. Warranties of accuracy by preparers and company officials.

In addition to the substantive issues surrounding requirements for full feasibility studies, administrative procedures for the ISA will be required including:

1. Review and approval of full feasibility study by ISA:
   a. Procedure and time for review and approval.
   b. Requests for presentation or further information.
   c. Approval or refusal of full feasibility study.
   d. Form of approval and written notification.
2. Result of refusal of full feasibility study by ISA:
   a. Withdrawal of preference.
   b. Opportunity to cure.
   c. Dispute resolution.
   d. Relinquishment.
   e. Rehabilitation.
   f. Termination.

After the feasibility study is approved by the ISA, the company is eligible to apply for a tenured mining licence.

5. Fiscal Regime Consideration for Polymetallic Nodule Exploitation

Fiscal Mandate under the United Nations Convention on the Law of the Sea

The ISA approach to a fiscal regime for seabed mining is set out in Section 8 (Financial Terms of Contracts) of the Implementing Agreement. Among other things, Section 8 establishes a framework of principles to be used as a basis for creating the financial terms of contracts between mining companies and the Authority. These principles (in paraphrase) include:

1. Payments to the Authority shall be fair both to the contractor and to the Authority and shall provide adequate means of determining compliance by the contractor with such system.

2. Rates of payments under the system shall be within the range of those prevailing in respect of land-based mining of the same or similar minerals.

3. The system should not be complicated and should not impose major administrative costs on the Authority or on a contractor.

4. Consideration should be given to the adoption of a royalty system or a combination of a royalty and profit-sharing system.

5. If alternative systems are decided upon, the contractor has the right to choose the system applicable to its contract. Any subsequent change in choice between alternative systems, however, shall be made by agreement between the Authority and the contractor.

6. Provision for an annual fixed fee shall be payable from the date of commencement of commercial production. This fee shall be established by the Council and may be credited against other payments due under the system.

7. The system of payments may be revised periodically in the light of changing circumstances. Any changes shall be applied in a non-discriminatory manner. Such changes may apply to existing contracts only at the election of the contractor.

Implications of the Mandate

Land-based minerals have historically been taxed in two ways: through payment of royalties, and as part of a country's general business income tax system. Since the 1970s additional forms of mineral taxation have begun to emerge. These new taxation schemes appeared first in developing countries and more recently in industrial nations including Australia. The new taxes range from the Indonesian and Philippine production sharing agreements to various forms of additional profits taxes based on the concept of economic rents. It is important to understand that in all land-based mineral fiscal schemes the only levy that is independent of production and capital costs is the mineral royalty.

Both normal business income taxes and the non-traditional tax approaches - including production sharing or economic rent taxes - are ultimately assessed based on some definition of investor cost and profits. In the case of the production sharing agreements popular in Southeast Asia, operating and capital costs are recovered through assignment of a (compensating) fraction of mine production to the mining company. Once this cost compensation has been made, any surplus production ('profit product') is divided between the country and mining company based on a predetermined split.

Although this system is often seen as an attractive alternative to traditional mining tax schemes, it still requires a system for identifying and deducting costs (both operating costs and capital) from revenues, and for determining profits.

To base a fiscal system for seabed minerals entirely on revenue-based royalties would result in rates that are several times those charged on land-based resources. This would almost certainly be a major mistake in terms both of optimum resource development and optimum investment and tax flows. A royalty-only system would greatly increase investor risk and result in development of only the highest-grade deposits. The obvious conclusion is that a tax-like infrastructure (including incorporating rules, procedures and administrative staff, audits, legal decisions) for determining project profits must be part of the seabed mining fiscal system, if optimum resource development and financial flows are to be achieved.

A second major characteristic of modern tax schemes relevant to the Seabed tax question is that most mineral tax systems are based entirely on national sovereignty.[1] There are few, if any, examples of international harmonization of mineral tax regimes on which to base the appropriateness of possible seabed fiscal systems. Given the range of minerals that might be subject to seabed mining, this means that in order to meet the comparability test contained in the Law of the Sea Treaty, there are a very large number of potential terrestrial fiscal schemes to be evaluated.

Finally, any eventual scheme must be theoretically and practically defensible. Some alternatives will be strongly opposed by investors, and retard development, while others may be criticized for undervaluing this common heritage resource. While criticism is inevitable the ideas on which the scheme is based must be transparent, understandable, and built upon some sort of theoretical concept. It would also be very useful if the proposed regime could present supporting empirical evidence about potential impacts.

Therefore, while protracted negotiations between stakeholders are inevitable, a fiscal system derived entirely from a negotiated agreement is probably not a satisfactory basis for a marine minerals fiscal policy.

Prerequisites to Formulating a Fiscal System for Marine Mining

Three basic premises were suggested from the background section:

1. The need to raise revenue from mining profits.

2. The need to meet the Section 8 requirement, "rates of payments under the system shall be within the range of those prevailing in respect of land-based mining of the same or similar minerals."

3. The need to establish a system based on economic principles and publically perceived as a fair and equitable sharing of the benefits from seabed mineral extraction.

In this section we will probe these premises further.

Need for mechanism to raise revenue from profits - The United Nations does not appear to a system comparable to the business income taxation system used by most of its member states. The lack of such a cost accounting tax code is a fundamental barrier to establishing a fiscal system for two reasons. First, it forces the ISA to focus solely on royalties based on physical quantities (unit-based royalties) or on revenue-based royalties (value-based royalties). Such total dependence will result in receipts that do not reflect the value of marine resources to investors and that are likely to create major distortions in resource investment or resource extraction rates. There is a rich literature on the impacts of inappropriately set royalty rates on mining practices (resource extraction), for example Otto, J. *et al.* (2006). Second, while not all mineral-rich countries have royalties, we were unable to find examples of countries that only had royalty-based fiscal systems. As a result it will be very difficult to meet the comparability provisions with a royalty-only system.

Since the UN lacks a business taxation infrastructure, it must either create one or simply adopt one from a member state. Neither alternative is satisfactory. Presumably, there are professional accountant groups that have developed model business taxation schemes that might be used as a guide for the ISA but, because of their general applicability, such schemes may be overly cumbersome and contain provisions that are irrelevant to a specialized activity like the mining of marine minerals. Another option might be for the ISA to convene a panel of tax experts to design a simple tax code that provides - among other things - for an estimate of project income and profits. But such a tax code is only one part of the necessary tax infrastructure, and provision would also need to be made for tax auditing, detailed administrative procedures and periodic review. Further, although such a custom tax effort might be possible, its implementation would force companies to maintain a separate set of accounts for their seabed activities.[2] The administrative burden of such a custom code could become a serious issue and, of course, would clash with the Section 8 provision suggesting that "the system should not be complicated and should not impose major administrative costs on the Authority or on a contractor."

The option of borrowing an existing business tax scheme from a member state is another possibility that might be explored. Presumably, the borrowed tax code would be from a member state with a large and highly diversified minerals industry that included most of the major mining companies and minerals that might be extracted from marine deposits. But existing tax codes in industrial mineral producing countries commonly reflect a number of historical policy changes, tax loopholes and compromises with special interest groups, and they are almost never theoretically defendable. Business tax codes in developing countries are often much

simpler but they are designed for smaller local companies and might require extensive modification for large-scale marine mining enterprises. While it is tempting to suggest that a full blown business tax code infrastructure is not needed for the purposes of a marine minerals fiscal package, this would have to be demonstrated by tax professionals with international experience and some knowledge of the special characteristics of mining.

Comparability - The Section 8 provision for comparable tax rates on similar minerals mined on land may have sounded straightforward to the Law of the Sea negotiators but in practice, comparability is a complicated question. Every mineral-producing nation has its own fiscal regime. Given the large number of sovereign jurisdictions and the wide variety of fiscal approaches to land-based mining, comparisons will need to be made on some secondary or derivative measure such as an 'effective tax rate'. Moreover, business income tax systems normally operate at company rather than project level. As a result, income or losses from non-mining activities may make it very difficult to find direct terrestrial comparisons.

Finally, the interaction of royalty and income tax payments sometimes differs between industrial and developing country mineral producers. While most countries view the payment of royalties by mines as a legitimate deduction from business income, it is common in the developing world to find reference to the 'government's take' from mining projects, which lumps together royalties, business taxes and (sometimes) other revenue streams from mining.[3]

To narrow the comparability field, we started our examination by considering the potential minerals (Table 4) that might be exploited by marine mining generally, rather than simply those minerals associated with polymetallic nodules. We found the following general inventory.

Table 4: Potential Minerals Subject to Seabed Authority Fiscal Regime

Types of Deposits	Minerals
Polymetallic nodules	Nickel, copper, cobalt and manganese
Manganese Crusts	Mainly cobalt, some vanadium, molybdenum and platinum

World trade in these minerals comes from land-based deposits in the main industrial mining countries (United States, Australia, Canada and Russian Federation) and from heavily mineralized middle-income nations including South Africa, Indonesia, Brazil, Chile and Peru.[4] The production of these minerals is heavily concentrated in the hands of a few major multinational mining countries although national companies play an important role in a few parts of the world. *For the purpose of this paper we defined "comparability with land-based mining of the same or similar minerals" in terms of these major producing areas and companies.* Before considering these comparisons it is useful to present a short description of a few major conceptual ideas that have dominated the design of mineral taxation schemes for several decades.

Concepts of Importance to a Fiscal System

Royalty

Royalty Guidance in the Seabed Mining Treaty - The basic guidance embodied in AGXI is sketchy and defines royalty in terms of royalty levels common to terrestrial mineral extraction. In the eyes of the negotiators of the royalty provisions, this phrase probably implied the assessment method most commonly used around the world, for example, a tax calculated as a percentage of the value (market price [5] multiplied by the weight of the mineral) of the mined commodities. While even this simple idea involves numerous definitional and administrative issues, it is common to both developing and industrial countries. Likewise, the drafters probably had in mind royalty levels in the 1 to 5 per cent range, which is common in many mining jurisdictions. However, there are also a large number of alternative royalty formulations in use around the world. These alternative formulations often reflect different definitions of the rationale behind the royalty charge.

Alternative Definitions and Calculation of Royalty - Most definitions of royalty payments involve concepts for: a) transferring ownership of minerals; or b) conferring a right to mine or develop mineral deposits. In practice, royalties are usually levied without regard to project profitability while taxes normally reflect some reference to profits.

There are three general conceptual approaches to royalty assessment: unit-based, value-based, and profit- or income-based. In addition, some jurisdictions have chosen to combine more than one approach into hybrid schemes. Each approach has its own specialized computational methods and definitions that are used to calculate the amount of royalty payable. In general, the administration of the royalty scheme is related to a number of variables in the calculation: unit value royalties require only information about the weight or volume of material being mined; revenue-based royalties require supplemental information on metal prices (and, perhaps, non-mining related costs); and income-based royalties which, in addition to weight and value information, also require information about mining costs and, commonly, some notion of project profits.

Unit-based royalties that are assessed at a fixed fee based on volume or weight are most commonly used in bulk commodities such as iron ore, coal and industrial minerals such as aggregate or sand and gravel. *Ad valorem* royalties are based on the value or revenue generated from mineral sales and are sometimes used with base and precious metal minerals. Profit-based royalties are most common in high-value minerals such as diamonds and gemstones.

The common approach is to make the determination of the royalty rate as transparent and administratively straightforward as possible. To the degree that government discretion is exercised, it is usually in favor of the mining company and involves such actions as the waiving or deferral of royalty payments due to adverse or extraordinary situations. For example, a prolonged labour strike or natural disaster might trigger a request by the mining company for temporary deferral of royalty payments to a host government.

Transparency in the calculation of mineral royalties is essential but where the form of the mineral changes (for example, mineral concentrates are smelted and refined) or where polymetallic mineral deposits are exploited, the calculations can become complex. Similarly, in cases where an integrated mining company develops or sells its production to an affiliated company, questions of 'arm's length' transfer prices can become contentious. In the case of marine minerals, the ultimate royalty scheme will have to address both the polymetallic concentrate question, and potentially, the transfer pricing issue.

It is important to recognize that the likely products of seabed mining (polymetallic concentrates) present inherent valuation problems, which complicate development of a fiscal system in several ways. First, they complicate price determination for royalty and profit calculations. Second, they complicate the Section 8 principle that "rates of payments under the system shall be within the range of those prevailing in respect of land-based mining of the same or similar minerals." This occurs since there may be relatively few terrestrial mining ventures that process comparable mineral products. Third, they present some difficulty in insuring that

mineral sales occur as 'arm's length' transactions since only a limited number of processing facilities will be available for smelting and refining the concentrates, and some of these facilities may be part of the vertically integrated mining operations recovering the seabed minerals. None of these problems are insurmountable but the notion of an administratively simple fiscal package may not be easily achieved.

Royalty as a Potential Environmental Tax - In considering approaches to a fiscal system for seabed minerals it is useful to make distinctions between the objectives of mineral policy for terrestrial and seabed mineral mining. First is the Common Heritage of Mankind ownership question. The ISA represents the collective interest of all peoples and countries in how the mineral potential of the oceans is exploited. In contrast, sovereign governments represent the interests of only those people living or born in a geographically defined area. This is a potentially important distinction for issues that are linked to basic mining operations. For example, even under the best of intentions and using the best technology, seabed mining is inherently destructive to the seabed and parts of the water column. While similar environmental destruction occurs with land-based mines, they are directly under the control of individual sovereign governments that represent the interests of only their citizens. Mining pollution from terrestrial mining operations certainly sometimes crosses international borders but in most cases disputes are resolved under well-established protocols and seldom involve the interests of distant nations. The environmental implications of seabed mining under the common heritage concept is complicated and is comparable only to the emerging issues surrounding international greenhouse gas regulation.[6] If environmental degradation of the marine ecosystem is inherent in seabed mining and if remediation is not practical or technologically possible, the logical alternative is financial compensation for the environmental damage and loss of ecosystem services from the seabed. While compensation might take place under the royalties and fees provisions in the UNCLOS Treaty, this approach is quite different from the logic used to justify royalties in terrestrial mining agreements.

Concept of 'Economic Rents'

In the early 1800s the British economist David Ricardo published his concept of 'economic rent'. While Ricardo's work focused on agricultural examples, later economic theorists extended the concepts to other sectors. One of the explanations of the application of economic rents theory most relevant to mineral taxation was contained in a 1995 article by mineral economist John Cordes (Cordes, 1995) at the Colorado School of Mines, which argued that economic rent is the difference between the market price for a mineral and the amount that owners of the mineral would be willing to accept. In other words, it is a surplus that is above the minimal financial return required for the investment. The important thing about this rent 'surplus' is that it can be taxed without changing the decisions of mining investors. In Cordes' words, "Economic rent could be taxed away without causing the pattern of resource use to be altered." [7] A simple example of an economic rent would be the windfall profits that result from speculation in the prices of precious metals like gold. Gold mining companies would reap this speculative additional revenue without any change in their operations or investment decisions.

A number of economic rent-based taxes have been proposed for the extractive sector. The closest approaches have been efforts in countries such as the Philippines and Papua New Guinea (now repealed) to levy an additional profits tax based on a calculation that seeks to determine: a) whether a profit threshold has been reached; and b) all amounts that exceed a defined internal rate of return, to which a tax rate is then applied. [8]

In Ghana a sliding scale royalty scheme is designed to reflect a resource rent approach by adjusting royalty by the ratio of costs-to-profits. Although interest in resource rent taxation has declined in the mining industry, the 'resource rent / additional profits' approach is still sometimes used in the petroleum industry.

Effective Tax Rates

The term 'effective tax rate' is increasingly used to describe the actual percentage tax liability of a taxpayer. It is not limited to mineral or petroleum tax analysis and, in fact, is probably more common in discussing the tax obligations of individuals rather than corporations. The effective tax rate is in contrast to the 'nominal' or 'headline' tax rates specified in government tax codes. It is determined by dividing the tax paid by the taxable income in a particular year. The effective tax rate is useful because it provides a realistic metric for understanding the amount of the actual taxes paid after allowing for all deductions, credits and other factors affecting tax liability. It allows for comparisons across time periods and between different tax jurisdictions.

The most important point for our current discussion is that the effective tax rate for a mining *company* and for a mining *project* (by the same company) is often substantially different. This is simply because the company's portfolio of projects includes some highly profitable ventures and some less profitable ventures, which are spread over several countries that may have more or less attractive tax schemes. A 2004 study, reprinted in the World Bank Royalty book, estimated the effective tax rate and investor's internal-rate-of-return for a model copper mine in several countries. The summary table from this study is presented below.

Table 5:   Study Results: Comparative Economic Measures for a Model Copper Mine in Selected Jurisdictions

Country	Foreign Investors IRR (%)	Total Effective Tax Rate (%)
Lowest Taxing quartile		
Sweden	15.7	28.6
Western Australia	12.7	36.4
Chile	15.0	36.6
Argentina	13.9	40.0
China	12.7	41.7
Second lowest taxing		
Papua New Guinea (2002)	13.3	42.7
Bolivia	11.4	43.1
South Africa	13.5	45.0
Philippines	13.5	45.3
Indonesia (7th CoW)	12.5	46.1
Kazakhstan	12.9	46.1
Second highest taxing		
Peru (2003)	11.7	46.5
Tanzania	12.4	47.8
Poland	11.0	49.6
Arizona (U.S.)	12.6	49.9
Mexico	11.3	49.9
Greenland	13.0	50.2
Highest taxing quartile		
Indonesia (non–CoW)	11.2	52.2
Ghana	11.9	54.4
Mongolia (2003)	10.6	55.0
Uzbekistan	9.3	62.9
Côte d'Ivoire	8.9	62.4
Ontario (Canada)	10.1	63.8

(Otto *et. al.*, 2006)

In contrast, the effective tax rates for major multinational mining *companies* show much lower effective tax rates. Empirical data on the effective tax rate of the major companies with substantial terrestrial production of potential marine minerals is presented in Table 6.

Table 6:   Effective Tax Rates of Major Companies Mining Terrestrial Deposits of Minerals of Potential Interest for Marine Mining

Company	Effective Tax Rate (%)			
	2006	2007	2008	AVG
BHP-Billiton	27.3	27.7	28.9	28.0
Rio Tinto	31.5	23.3	25.3	46.0
Anglo American	28.9	27.6	30.5	28.6
Xstrata-Inco	45.4	28.7	25.2	33.2
Vale (CVRD)	18.3	21.0	4.0	14.4
Average	28.4	26.6	25.7	

Source: (Price Waterhouse Coopers, 2009).

Table 6 shows that – with the notable exception of the Brazilian company VALE (CVRD) – all of the identified companies were paying effective tax rates approaching or exceeding 30 per cent for the three-year period 2006-2008.[9]

By inference we can assume that an effective tax rate at company level would broadly be acceptable to most potential marine mining companies but would be substantially below the effective tax rate for new land-based *projects* in a number of terrestrial jurisdictions. In other words, the area where both company and new project comparability must be reconciled involves an effective tax rate (including royalties) of 35 to 45 per cent.[10]

Summary Observations

As early ventures mature, the need to develop a fiscal package for marine mining is becoming increasingly important. The framework for such a fiscal package was anticipated in the original Law of the Sea Convention and, subsequently, in AGXI. While the framework is reasonably clear and consistent, it is not easily implemented and does not lend itself to definitive analysis. Three issues are particularly problematic: the setting of fiscal rates based on comparable land-based minerals; the problem of identifying a tax and cost accounting code on which fiscal calculations can be made; and the concept that a simple system can be developed that does not burden the ISA or mining investors. This paper has tried to

elaborate these issues and suggest possible avenues for future investigations but, in many ways, has only scratched the surface of what may be involved in preparing a defendable ISA fiscal policy for marine mining.

The whole fiscal question is clouded by the nature of private sector participants in the value chain of mining and processing marine minerals. Most of the ideas and fiscal concepts discussed in this paper are based on the world's land-based mining industry operating at arm's length in a free market environment. However, since many of the marine minerals are of strategic importance to economic development in rapidly emerging nations including China, India and Brazil, the current mining industry model may not be totally appropriate.

Finally, the responsibility to protect the common heritage of mankind creates its own special problem for mining policy. These responsibilities can be most easily seen in two areas: inevitable environmental damage; and a sort of fiduciary responsibility to ISA stakeholders, particularly people in poor nations who may receive some financial benefits from future mining of the seabed. The fact that seabed mining will not be a public enterprise directly raises questions about how to appropriately divide both profit and risk. This, in turn, raises difficult resource rent questions about capturing windfall profits and rents in the name of social justice. Both environmental destruction and the division of rents must somehow be accommodated in the eventual fiscal package.

Notes

1.   There is a long (and increasing) tradition of having royalty receipts accrue to local, state or provincial authorities. Local authorities also commonly impose their own state or provincial business income taxes on mining ventures. This local revenue sharing creates a further potential complication in determining an appropriate comparative model for seabed taxation.

2.   This may not be a major concern for large transnational companies, which are often faced with maintaining separate accounts for each jurisdiction in which they operate, but it could be a considerable burden for domestically oriented firms.

3.   Some jurisdictions also impose other taxes. Other revenue sources might include such items as dividends from equity participation or taxes on repatriated profits. In addition, state/ provincial/ local taxes are common in industrial countries.

4.   Production figures should not be confused with mineral abundance since exploration is very unevenly distributed worldwide, particularly in developing nations.

5.   With or without specific deductions to cover costs involving in transportation, processing or marketing.

6.   Fisheries management issues certainly involve common heritage questions but are largely addressed only by subgroups of the international community (for example fishing nations or regional organizations or species-specific commissions).

7.   It is important not to confuse 'rents' with the compensation for the services of labour, capital, and entrepreneurship. Taxing these payments reduces the incentives for resource owners to provide their services to the market, and so distorts the behavior and performance of the economy.

8.   While our original list of multinational companies included the French company ERMAT the PriceWaterhouseCoopers Study did not include an effective tax rate estimate for this important nickel / manganese producer.

9.   If it were decided that royalty rates (accruing to state or provincial authorities) should be paid in addition to the effective tax rate, the starting point for the fiscal package would increase to, say, 35%.

10.   The 45% project tax rate reflects the midpoint in second lowest taxing quartile (Table 2).

6. Polymetallic Nodule Commodities: Development, Supply and Demand and Market Considerations

Overview

Since the first consideration of commercial exploitation of deep seabed PN the future of the industry has been primarily dependent on the economics of three major metals - copper, nickel, cobalt and to a lesser extent manganese.[1] The economics of the individual metal markets have in turn been largely dependent on global economic growth, diversification, innovation and the resulting increased levels of supply and demand. These relationships remain substantially consistent and are operational today. As a result, almost a decade of rising demand and prices for mineral commodities has resulted in increased interest and activity with respect to the development of new sources of mineral supply. This has translated into a renewed interest in the potential exploitation of deep seabed mineral resources overall, and in manganese nodules and polymetallic massive sulphides. This increased interest is reflected in terms of both: a) an increased number of new prospecting and exploration applications to the ISA; and b) an expansion and diversification of applicants.

As the ISA proceeds with the development of a deep seabed PN mineral exploitation regime, anticipated to be in place by 2015, the drivers and links between economic development, commodity demand, commodity prices and investment are of critical importance to the ISA. Among the key issues that will need to be considered are:

1. Present status of PN metals nickel, copper, cobalt.

2. Intermediate- to medium-term supply and demand issues concerning copper, nickel, cobalt.

3. Lag and lead times between metal prices and industry response.

4. Industry response to changes in the metal markets.

The following brief overview of present reserves, resources, production and markets (largely taken from the USGS Mineral and commodity fact books) is presented as background for the following discussions on medium- to long-term PN metal developments.

Nickel

Approximately 80 per cent of the primary nickel consumed in 2011 was used in alloys, such as stainless steel and super alloys. Because nickel increases an alloy's resistance to corrosion and its ability to withstand extreme temperatures, equipment and parts made of nickel-bearing alloys are often used in harsh environments, such as those in chemical plants, petroleum refineries, jet engines, power generation facilities, and offshore installations. Nickel alloys are increasingly being used in making rechargeable batteries for portable computers, power tools, and hybrid and electric vehicles. Nickel is also plated onto such items as bathroom fixtures to reduce corrosion and provide an attractive finish.

Global nickel production and reserves are shown in Table 7 and show that Australia and New Caledonia have by far the world's largest reserves. However the Russian Federation, followed by Indonesia, the Philippines and Canada dominate production.

Table 7:   World Nickel Mine Production and Reserves
            (Data in metric tons of nickel content unless otherwise noted)

| Country | Mine Production (tonnes) | | Reserves |
	2010	2011	
United States	–	–	–
Australia	170,000	180,000	24,000,000
Botswana	28,000	32,000	490,000
Brazil	59,100	83,000	8,700,000
Canada	158,000	200,000	3,300,000
Colombia	72,000	72,000	720,000
Cuba	70,000	74,000	5,000,000
Dominican Republic	–	14,000	1,000,000
Indonesia	232,000	230,000	3,900,000
Madagascar	15,000	25,000	1,600,000
New Caledonia	130,000	140,000	12,000,000
Philippines	173,000	230,000	1,100,000
Russian Federation	269,000	280,000	6,000,000
South Africa	40,000	42,000	3,700,000
Other countries	99,000	100,000	4,600,000
World total (rounded)	1,590,000	1,800,000	80,000,000

(USGS, 2012 a,b)

The comparatively low nickel prices of 2009 increased dramatically in 2010 largely because of the growth in demand and production of stainless steel: about 70 per cent of global nickel supply is used in the production of stainless steel in China, Japan, Europe, the United States and other industrial countries. However, almost as quickly as it rose in 2010, the growth in stainless steel consumption slowed to approximately 5 per cent in 2011. As demand decreased for nickel there was a corresponding decrease in nickel prices. However, despite falling inventories and still positive demand gains, nickel prices came under additional pressure because of the expected surge in new nickel projects - the largest being in Brazil, Madagascar, New Caledonia and Papua New Guinea - but increases were also expected in Australia, Canada and elsewhere. These developments are in addition to existing mining capacities as shown in Tables 8 and 9.
The new capacity from these projects will include traditional nickel sulphides, ferro-

nickel and laterite high pressure acid leach (HPAL) projects, and Chinese nickel pig iron (NPI). Although HPAL projects have had considerable technical problems and delays in recent years they appear ready to begin operations.

It is worth noting that the Chinese NPI industry developed as a result of the nickel price boom in the mid- 2000s, with the import of nickel laterite ores from Indonesia and the Philippines. However, Indonesia has proposed developing its own NPI industry and is considering banning nickel ore exports from 2014, which could reduce China's output. NPI production is relatively expensive and may serve a longer-term floor to prices.

Nickel prices are expected to decline due to the substantial supply additions in the near future, and are likely to reflect production costs in the medium term.

Copper

Copper's chemical, physical and aesthetic properties make it the material of choice in a wide range of domestic, industrial and high tech applications. Alloyed with other metals, such as zinc (to form brass), aluminum or tin (to form bronzes), or nickel, it can acquire new characteristics for use in highly specialized applications. Global copper production and reserves are shown in Table 8.

Table 8:   World Copper Mine Production and Reserves
(Data in thousand metric tons of copper content unless otherwise noted)

	Mine Production (tonnes)		
	2010	2011	Reserves
United States	1,100	1,120	35,000
Australia	870	940	86,000
Canada	525	550	7,000
Chile	5,420	5,420	190,000
China	1,190	1,190	30,000
Democratic Republic of the Congo	343	440	20,000
Kazakhstan	380	360	7,000
Mexico	260	365	38,000
Peru	1,250	1,220	90,000
Poland	425	425	26,000
Russian Federation	703	710	30,000
Zambia	690	715	20,000
Other countries	1,900	2,200	80,000
World total (rounded)	15,900	16,100	690,000

(USGS, 2012a,b)

The lowest copper grade acceptable for mining feasibility depends on the quality of the deposit. For underground deposits the lowest feasible grades are between 1.2 to 2 per cent copper content. For open pit mining the lowest feasible grade is about 0.5 per cent copper content. For copper deposits containing valuable by-products, the grades acceptable for open pit mining can be as low as 0.25 to 0.3 per cent copper content.

Copper prices began rising in late 2003 due to strong demand, falling stocks and the impact of earlier capacity closures when prices were low. Strong Chinese demand growth has been the main contributor to rising prices. However, numerous supply shortfalls - due to strikes, technical problems, lower ore grades, and delays bringing on new capacity - have kept stocks chronically low, and propelled prices to record nominal highs in 2006.

Copper consumption growth in the first ten months of 2011 fell slightly after an 11 per cent gain in 2010. China's apparent demand (excluding stock changes) slowed sharply from 2010, but given likely destocking, actual consumption was probably higher (China's copper imports picked up in the second half of the year suggesting an end to inventory withdrawal). In the Organisation for Economic Co-operation and Development (OECD), strong demand growth at the start of the year turned sharply negative, and growth elsewhere turned slightly negative.

Refined metal prices in recent years have taken their toll on consumption, as users substituted copper with other materials, such as aluminum and plastics, and lowered the copper content in applications.

Copper prices have remained well above the costs of production because of continued problems at the mine supply level, including slower than expected ramp-up at new mines, technical problems at existing operations, declining ore grades, strikes, accidents and adverse weather. Many of these incidents have occurred in Chile, which supplies 35 per cent of the world's mined copper.

Over the medium term, copper prices are expected to decline as demand moderates and new capacity pushes the market into modest surplus. However, growth in new global capacity is underway, with new capacity from numerous medium-sized projects expected to come online from 2012, as well as the massive Oyu Tolgoi project in Mongolia, which will add significant growth in 2013-14.

Cobalt

Cobalt is used primarily in the manufacture of super alloys, which are corrosion-resistant alloys that retain their strength at very high temperatures. Gas turbine engines and other components used in aircraft and space vehicles, chemical and petroleum plants, and power plants depend on the high temperature strength of super alloys. Cobalt also has impressive magnetic properties that it retains at temperatures as high as 1,121°C. Cobalt is an important component of the magnets used in computer disc drives and electric motors, helping them operate more efficiently at a wide range of temperatures. The leading global use of cobalt is in rechargeable batteries used in mobile phones, portable computers, and hybrid and electric vehicles to help increase battery life and stability and to reduce corrosion.

World cobalt production for 2010 and 2012 and national reserves are shown in Table 9, which shows that the Central African copper belt constitutes almost half of the world's reserves of cobalt. Assuming a world market for cobalt of approximately 100,000 tonnes per annum, the Democratic Republic of the Congo (DRC) and its copper industry may well be the major producers of cobalt for the foreseeable future.

Cobalt supply is influenced by economic, environmental, political and technological factors affecting exploration for and production of copper, nickel and other metals, as well as diverse factors specific to the cobalt industry. Until the 1990s the world's cobalt production was dominated by the DRC and Zambia.

During the late 1990s and early 2000, when mining of copper-cobalt deposits in the DRC was restricted because of regional conflict and lack of investment in that country's mining sector, Co production shifted largely to Australia and Canada with: 50 per cent of cobalt production provided by the global nickel industry (sulphide and laterite producers); 35 per cent by the copper industry and others; and 15 per cent by primary cobalt producers.

However, beginning in 2003 changes in the structure of the DRC mining policy regarding cobalt and copper led to increasing exploration and development that continued intermittently through 2008. Since 2008 cobalt production in the DRC has increased dramatically as has investment in the nation's copper industry, but developments are underway that will significantly increase production (Table 10).

Table 9: World Cobalt Mine Production and Reserves
(Data in metric tons of cobalt content unless otherwise noted)

Country	2010	2011	Reserves
United States	-	-	-
Australia	3,850	4,000	1,400,000
Brazil	1,600	1,700	87,000
Canada	4,600	7,200	130,000
China	6,500	6,500	80,000
Democratic Republic of the Congo	47,400	52,000	3,400,000
Cuba	3,600	3,600	500,000
Morocco	-	2,500	20,000
New Caledonia	1,000	2,000	370,000
Russian Federation	6,200	6,300	250,000
Zambia	5,700	5,700	270,000
Other Countries	6,800	7,000	990,000
World total (rounded)	89,500	98,000	7,500,000

Source: USGS, 2012

CRU has forecast that prices will average US$14.00/lb over 2012 due to a combination of refined surplus and high levels of inventories of raw materials in China. Looking ahead, continuing annual surpluses in the refined market will weigh on prices in the medium term, with prices slightly below US$13.00/lb in 2014. In the longer term, CRU projects that cobalt prices will strengthen to approximately US$17.00/lb in 2017, when the refined market is predicted to turn to a deficit.

Table 10: Planned cobalt production increases in the Democratic Republic of the Congo

	Mine	Projected Output
1.	Tenke Fungurume (Freeport McMoran)	8,000 tpa cydroxide cobalt
2.	KOL Luilu refinery (Glencore)	8,000 tpa cobalt cathode
3.	Ruashi (Metorex)	3,500 tpa as hydroxide
4.	Mukondo (Camec)	5,000 tpa as cathode
5.	Mutanda (Glencore)	9,000 tpa as hydroxide
6.	Klowezi Tailings (First Quantum)	7,000 tpa as hydroxide
7.	Shituru Refinery (Gecamines)	7,000 tpa as low grade cathode
8.	Etoile (Chemaf)	6,000 tpa as cathode
9.	Deziwa (Ex Copperbelt Minerals)	4,500 tpa as hydroxide

Wilburn, 2011

Of particular importance to the ISA is the fact that the planned expansion of DRC cobalt and copper mining and processing capacities brings the distinct possibility of an oversupply of cobalt, which may have a major impact on the economics of near-term PN exploitation as well as on longer term cobalt-rich manganese crusts within the Area.

Manganese

Manganese is an essential industrial metal used as an additive in a wide range of steels, nonferrous alloys, and electronic components, as well as in specialty chemical applications. In the steel manufacturing process, the addition of manganese removes impurities such as sulphur and oxygen. It also optimizes the physical properties of the steel by improving its strength, hardness, and abrasion resistance. Of the roughly 15 million tonnes (mt) of manganese metal produced annually (Table 11), roughly 89 per cent is upgraded into alloyed manganese and foundry products. The remaining 11 per cent of manganese ore is consumed in the production of metallurgical and chemical products, including electrolytic manganese metal (EMM), electrolytic manganese dioxide (EMD), lithium manganese oxide, manganese sulfate, and other chemicals.

World Resources -Land-based manganese *reserves* are large but irregularly distributed (Table 11). South Africa possesses about 75 per cent of the world's identified manganese reserves with the Ukraine and Brazil each having approximately 10 per cent of the world's reserves.

Manganese Prices - From US$0.36 per pound in 2002, monthly EMM prices rose more than sixfold to $2.41 in June 2007, averaging roughly $1.76 per pound until the fourth quarter of 2008. This rapid rise in price was largely fueled by demand for manganese in rapidly developing China, which presently accounts for roughly 85 per cent of global demand. Although declining in 2009, to roughly US$1.00 per pound, prices trended generally upward to US$1.53 at the end of 2011. Many of the underlying fundamentals that have driven manganese prices, namely rising production costs, more stringent Chinese regulations and strong demand growth, remain intact.

Table 11:   World Manganese Mine Production and Reserves
(Data in thousand metric tons gross weight unless otherwise specified)

	Mine Production		
	2010	2011	Reserves
United States	–	–	–
Australia	3,100	2,400	93,000
Brazil	780	1,000	110,000
China	2,600	2,800	44,000
Gabon	1,420	1,500	21,000
India	1,000	1,100	56,000
Mexico	175	170	4,000
South Africa	2,900	3,400	150,000
Ukraine	540	340	140,000
Other countries	1,340	1,400	Small
World total (rounded)	13,900	14,000	630,000

Source USGS, 2012

Polymetallic Nodule Commodities: Development, Supply and Demand and Market Considerations

The CPM Group (CPM, 2011, 2012) estimates that EMM real prices may average US$1.72 between 2012 and 2016 and in real prices may reach US$2.11 on an annual basis by the second half of the period. In the longer term, it is forecast that over the next 10 years real electrolytic manganese metal prices will average $1.92 per pound, reaching an annual high of $2.30 in 2021. This is nearly double the annual average price over the last 10 years.

Future Supply and Demand: Global supply and apparent demand of electrolytic manganese have historically been closely aligned. However, the increased demand for EMM between 2000 and 2007 resulted in a substantial and sustained shift in the market's dynamics with increased demand leading to increased supplies and ultimately to overcapacity. China's capacity in particular has increased nearly 16 fold in the last decade, leading to large-scale plant closures outside the country. The EMM market is highly concentrated with over 97 per cent of global EMM production sourced from China in 2010. South Africa, the only other EMM producing country, accounted for the remaining 3 per cent of global supply.

Increasing uncertainty with respect to China's EMM industry, because of falling ore grades, increased political pressure to reduce the environmental impact of the manganese industry and government policy on imports and exports, is expected to have a major impact on the EMM market in the next decade. After more than a decade of primarily depending on China experts expect new EMM capacity may come on-stream between 2013 and 2016 from five probable projects in the Ukraine, Gabon, Kazakhstan, Mexico and the United States. Other possible sources of EMM supply could come from development projects in Canada, Finland and the United States. During the second half of the forecast period China could at times become a small net importer.

Manganese, technology and China: Nickel, copper and cobalt have historically been the major metals of interest with respect to PN exploitation. The economic potential of manganese has also been recognized and has occasionally been considered in the financial analyses of nodule exploitation programmes. Most analyses of PN economics, however, do not consider manganese as a primary economic metal. This has largely been because of the relatively low grade of manganese in nodules compared to on-land deposits in South Africa (greater than 44 per cent manganese), or deposits that are essentially equal in grade but more accessible, such as those in the Ukraine.

Nevertheless, a huge quantity of residue is generated during the leaching process of roast-reduced manganese nodules (almost 70 per cent of the nodules treated), which contains a significant amount of manganese (about 26 per cent), iron (10 per cent) and silica (16 per cent). This residue can be classified as a low-grade manganese ore.

According to the US Bureau of Mines the leached residue cannot be directly employed for silicomanganese smelting due to a lower manganese/iron ratio (2:3) than is generally required. While the manganese/iron ration can be improved by blending the residue with manganese ore, higher-grade manganese ore must be used, as with existing low-grade manganese deposit materials, to produce silicomanganese, ferromanganese and other ferroalloys. The only major present consumer of such products is China, since an approximately 20 per cent low-grade ore is relatively high-grade ore compared to the approximately 10 per cent domestic ores presently utilized.

Conclusion: The residual low-grade manganese ore that results from the processing of nodules would at present be of major interest primarily for China and in the future possibly for other seabed mining nations with large-scale steel industries such as South Korea, India and Japan. For the ISA the primary concern will be to ensure that any downstream utilization of the residue from nodule processing for nickel, copper and cobalt is appropriately accounted for within the fiscal regime and in the determination of resource rents.

Intermediate to Medium-Term Supply and Demand Issues for Nickel, Copper, Cobalt

There are presently no major supply constraints for any of the key PN metals (copper, nickel or cobalt) largely because: a) capacity expansion within existing large-scale deposits, particularly for copper in South America and nickel and cobalt in Canada and the Russia Federation; b) 'pipe line' projects are already underway for nickel and cobalt; and c) an increasing number of areas and new deposits, both smaller high-grade and larger lower grade, are being reactivated or discovered (particularly nickel, copper and cobalt) in Africa. However, that is only part of the story.

In the intermediate term PN metal markets will continue to be demand-driven, as can be seen from the first half of 2012 where the economic outlook for growth has weakened, accompanied by a weakening of prices for nickel, copper and cobalt. If this weakening of prices continues it may well lead to longer term 'knock on' impacts such as those seen in the 1990 and early 2000s. For example, most mining companies make decisions to invest that are strongly influenced by current market conditions, which often further exacerbate the disequilibrium between supply and demand, especially with the long lead times needed to bring on new production.

This 'present view' short-sightedness of market-driven decisions makes it difficult for risk adverse mining companies to justify spending millions (and often billions) of dollars on new mining projects when prices are weak. A further complication, both for the intermediate and longer term is the issue of capital and operating cost inflation (Table 12), which is at its highest level ever.

Table 12: Recent examples of reported capital cost escalation in the copper mining sector

Year	Project	Country	Operator	Date	Prior Capex (US$M)	Date	Latest Capex (US$M)	US CAPCO Escalation
2011	Galore Creek	Canada	Teck Resources	2006	1800	2011	5200	189%
2012	Collahuasi expansion	Chile	Xstrata	2007	2450	2012	6500	165%
2011	Pascua Lama	Chile	Barrick Gold Corp	2009	2641	2011	5000	89%
2011	Udokan	Russian Federation	Baikal Mining	2008	3800	2011	7000	84%
2010	El Pachon	Argentina	Xstrata	2009	2400	2010	4100	71%
2011	Pebble	USA	Anglo American	2007	2800	2011	4690	68%
2011	Conga	Peru	Newmont Mining	2010	3382	2012	5000	48%

Polymetallic Nodule Commodities: Development, Supply and Demand and Market Considerations

2011	Cerro Casale	Chile	Barrick Gold Corp	2010	4181	2011	6000	43%
2012	Cobre Panama	Panama	Inmet	2009	4320	2012	6181	43%
2011	Andina Expansio	Chile	Codelco	2008	4750	2011	6400	35%
2010	Frieda River	PNG	Xstrata	2009	4200	2010	5300	26%
2010	Las Bambas	Peru	Xstrata	2009	3800	2010	4200	11%
2010	Tampakan	Philippines	Xstrata	2009	5650	2010	5900	4%

Source: Brook Hunt, Barclays Research

Increasing capital and operating costs increase investment uncertainty, leading to reduced project financing and ultimately to reduced supply.

The level of capital intensity needed for some types of mineral development, especially for copper and nickel mining, has risen to a very high level. For most companies this means that if project economics are to be viable, higher long-term price assumptions must be used. This is especially difficult to justify during periods, such as the present, when prices are falling and sentiment towards the short-run outlook is negative. This is of particular interest to the ISA in that it may drive potential investors towards smaller high-grade deposit development with a negative impact on both resource utilization and sustainability.

Mining company investment decisions are not expected to affect supply fundamentals in the short-term and the market will continue to be demand-driven. Therefore, it is to be expected that prices will decline in the medium-term for all PN metals primarily because of anticipated lower levels of global, regional (North America, OECD) and national (China and India in particular) economic growth.

However, in the intermediate to longer term there is a cumulative impact from the delays, which raise two fundamental questions:

1. Are current timetables for new base metals supply coming on stream realistic?

    a. The copper industry, for example, is still feeling the effects of the capital spending cuts and delays to new projects during the 2009-2011 financial crisis, with 1.4 mt of mine production not realized in 2011.

The trend for long-term copper supply is particularly noteworthy given that the copper market is expected to be particularly vulnerable to slippage in new mine supply over the next few years. This matters more for the medium-term outlook for nickel given the supply shortfalls of even current production schedules.

2. What is the effect of deferred development on potential PN metal developments?

    a. In the intermediate term it would be most likely to result in deferred development of PN exploitation within the Area. However, based on previous history it is expected that prices and profits will rise with renewed interest in nodule development in the longer term.

Although there will be some resource constraints in the future for key PN metals and metal prices, prices are expected to decrease only modestly in the long term. However, there are a number of other factors that many seriously impact upon the PN metals market. Among the most significant are: an overall decline in ore grades coupled with increasing mining and processing costs, and environmental and land rehabilitation costs in addition to increasing water and energy costs that may hold significant 'unpleasant surprise'.

Lag and Lead Times between Metal Prices and Industry response [2]

From the inception of active exploration and consideration of the exploitation potential of PN, the major determinant of possible exploitation continues to be the metal prices of the contained metals (nickel, copper, cobalt and to a lesser extent manganese). As metal prices have waxed and waned industry interest in possible exploitation has followed. For example, the low metal prices of the 1990s resulted in: a) relatively low levels of investment; b) in many cases the closing of high-cost producers, for example the lateritic deposits of the Philippines; c) deferred development of projects such as the Ramu Mine in Papua New Guinea; and d) a dramatic drop in interest in the possible exploitation of PN in the Area.

The commodity price boom of 2002 to 2008, the longest and strongest of the last fifty years, came at the end of a prolonged period of weak and declining real term prices. The strength of the demand and the resulting price rise was largely the result of two factors. First was the rapidly increasing demand for metals from China, the extent of which, in terms of both the quantity and the immediacy of demand, caught mining companies off guard.

Secondly, companies had had little incentive to invest in large-scale new capacity for many years (during the late 1990s and early 2000s the preoccupation of the industry was on cost-cutting and capital efficiency, not volume growth). The resulting increased demand rapidly outstripped supply, which in turn forced inventories to low levels and pushed production up against capacity constraints, further exacerbating the price rise. Equally important, because of relatively

low levels of exploration the metal industry had few 'shovel ready' projects in the pipeline. An additional and major contributing factor was the concurrent depreciation of the U.S. dollar.

In 2010 world metals consumption recorded an 11 per cent growth and it was widely anticipated that because of renewed and continuing strong demand in China and continuing capacity constraints, the prevailing cycle of high metal prices was likely to be longer and higher than previous cycles. However, metal prices fell from their highs in early 2011 as concerns about global growth increased as a result of: a) the ongoing US debt crises (depression), b) the rapidly evolving debt crises in some

OECD countries; and c) slowing growth and policy changes within China. Nevertheless prices rebounded slightly in mid-to-late 2011, particularly for copper, largely on the basis of: a) increased demand in China (including earlier re-stocking); b) lower stocks; c) production cutbacks; and d) global stocks (outside China) began to rise.

In 2012 all metals prices were well off their highs of early 2011 with: a) nickel prices declining by more than one third because of slowing demand by the stainless steel sector and expectations of large new nickel production capacity additions in 2012 and beyond; b) copper prices dropping by a quarter, but remaining above the costs of production due to supply tightness at the mine level; and c) the cobalt price declining by a fifth from its 2011 high. Nevertheless, previously exceptionally high metal prices have led to exceptional profitability, which has resulted in unprecedented levels of industry investment in exploration and development (estimated at approximately US$90 billion in 2012 for non-ferrous metals).

There are two additional issues to consider in terms of possible investment and exploitation of PN resources of the Area:

1. There is a 'lag' between price peaks and investment peaks (the decision to commit and arrange funding for the development

of a 'new deposit' or a 'brown field' project), which is normally from 3 to 5 years.

2. Once a commitment is made there is an additional lag of 3 to 7 years before mineral resources are extracted and can be placed on the market.[3]

Although there remains a great deal of uncertainty associated with potential commercial PN exploitation, it is useful to consider the above 'price-to-product' transitions in terms of potential PN exploitation in the Area and associated supply issues.

Industry Response to Changes in the Metal Markets

The outlook for PN commodity prices in the near term is uncertain, largely because of the inherent volatility of the market and the ensuing reactions of government and industry. There are long-term concerns about: the pace of demand in developing countries (particularly China and India); availability and access to supplies; technology developments; production costs; government policies; and environmental considerations.

Metal prices will ultimately depend on the ability of producers to vary capacity to meet demand. Rapid growth in demand that stretches capacity development will require sufficiently high prices to bring on adequate marginal capacity. Should demand be relatively weak, for example because of economic recession, prices may have to temporarily fall to the levels of shut-in capacity, for example, the operating costs of highest-cost producers. In the long term, prices are assumed to equate to long-run marginal costs (LRMC). Nevertheless there is expected to be a modest increase in the cost curve for most metals in real terms due to the rising costs for energy, labour and materials, which will remain partially in place when price cycles turn downward. Nickel prices may have a significant increase because of costly new technologies.

Demand for copper is expected to double over the next two decades with more than half of the growth occurring in China and India. Between 1990 and 1999, China accounted for 41 per cent of the growth in main metals consumption, increasing 4.2 mt or 13.2 per cent per annum. However, between 1999 and 2005, China accounted for nearly two thirds of the growth in global demand, as its volume growth more than doubled, increasing by 9.8 mt or 17.0 per cent per annum. China's rapid growth in metal demand had a significant impact on the recent rise in metals prices, particularly where it is a large net importer, in terms of PN minerals (copper, nickel, cobalt), iron ore, lead and zinc. These metals have increased most in price.

Further adding to industry uncertainty are the risks to metal demand, for example, for fiber optics and wireless technologies in telecommunications, plastic tube plumbing for construction; composite materials for jet aircraft; and plastic and glass bottles. Perhaps the greatest uncertainty arises from development itself that will bring even greater portions of the world's population into the per-capita income range where metals demand accelerates. Much of this demand has been fueled by investment in public infrastructure and manufacturing facilities for domestic and export consumption. There is significant potential for copper production to expand, led by North and South America. While Canada, Chile and Peru have the largest potential, other countries such as Brazil and Mexico and Australia also have good prospects, while Mongolia and the African copper belt (particularly the DR Congo and Zambia) offer the largest potential.

Projects are also expected in other countries that offer low-cost power from natural gas (for example, oil producing countries), and from hydropower (for example, Brazil, Canada and Norway). Until 2025, capacity will continue to be developed in regions with a low opportunity cost of power (for example a number of oil producing countries). Two regions that will struggle to add capacity are North America and Europe because of higher power costs, environmental regulations and prohibitive labour costs. China is not expected to be a location for export smelters in the long term because of expected upward pressures on power and labour costs, and appreciation of its currency.

There will be no shortage of metal resources over the next two decades and beyond. However, ores are likely to be of lower grade, and new projects are likely to be in more difficult locations, such as the deep seabed, thereby raising exploration and development costs. This will reinforce the upward shift in long-run marginal prices, as will the need for increasingly expensive infrastructure, new processing technology and the need to confront political risk.

High prices and profits will also entice workers to seek higher wages and prod host governments and communities to seek more equitable mineral taxation and benefit sharing arrangements. These can affect the development of new projects such as those in the deep seabed.

The industry has continued to make strides in reducing the cost of mining and smelting operations through technological developments and better project management. There have been dramatic expansions in mine capacity, notably of copper in Chile. Improved equipment and larger machinery have helped improve economies of scale at these locations. Occasionally major breakthroughs occur, for example the introduction of leaching technology in the production of copper and the development of pressure acid leach for the recovery of nickel from laterite deposits. It is expected that the industry will continue to strive to develop new technologies to reduce costs. The future holds many such challenges.

Notes

1. A number of additional metals, in particular molybdenum, platinum, and rare earth metals (REM) occur in non-economic concentrations and are therefore not normally included in economic analyses.

2. Although they should not be, longer-term price assumptions are often affected by current conditions. It was the conservative long-term price assumptions held by the industry and the mining companies that contributed to miners' slow investment response to the large increase in emerging market demand in the 2000s.

3. For example, a rise in copper prices in 1987 did not cause an acceleration in global mine production until 1995, and a decline in prices following the price peak of 1995 resulted in a reduction in global mine supply until 2002.

7. Manganese Nodule Economic Sensitivity Analysis

Overview

Because of their relatively high manganese, nickel, copper and cobalt content, the PN of the Area have been considered as a potential source of exploitable resources since the 1970s. As a result there has been continual prospecting, exploration and intermittent small-scale recovery, pilot scale processing and metallurgical testing and economic analysis to assess the potential of PN as an exploitable mineral resource. More comprehensive economic analyses of the economic viability of PN have been developed since the 1970s, and among the most recent studies are those of Andrews et al. (1983), Hillman and Gosling (1985)[,] Charles et al. (1990) and Soreide et al. (2001) (Table 13).

Table 13:   Comparison of economic evaluation of manganese nodule development

	Soreide et al. (2001) High-Temperature and High-Pressure Sulfuric Acid Leach Process			Hillman and Gosling (1985) Cuprion Ammoniacal Leach Process			Andrews et al. (1983) Reduction and Hydrochloric Acid Leach Process			Charles et al. (1990) Reduction and Hydrochloric Acid Leach Process		
	Mining (wet)	Trans. (dry)	Process. (dry)	Mining (wet)	Trans. (dry)	Process (dry)	Mining (wet)	Trans. (dry)	Process. (dry)	Mining (wet)	Trans. (dry)	Process. (dry)
Production (y)	1.1M	0.7M	0.7M	4.2M 300d/y	3.0M 300d/y	3.0M 330d/y	2.3M 300d/y	1.5M 300d/y	1.5M 330d/y	2.3M 250d/y	1.5M	1.5M
Capital cost	127M$	93M$	271M$	590M$	310M$	727M$	180M$	176M$	513M$	282M$	188M$	470M$
Capital cost ratio	26%	19%	55%	36%	19%	45%	21%	20%	59%	30%	20%	50%
Equity/loan	30:70			100:0			100:0			50:50		
Operating cost / loan interest / survey cost	21.8M$ 8% 1.9M$	13.5M$	22.9M$	77M$ 0% 3M$	37M$	111M$	45M$ 0% 6M$	25M$	165M$	48M$	36M$	156M$
Operating cost ratio	38%	23%	39%	34%	16%	50%	19%	11%	70%	20%	15%	65%
Metal	Prices $/lb	Recovery	Product t/y	Price $/lb	Recovery	Product t/y	Price $/lb	Recovery	Product t/y	Price $/lb	Recovery	Product t/y
	20.00	83%	2,652	8.53	65%	5,070	5.5	85%	3,375	6.8	85%	3,525
	3.33	98%	2,548	3.62	92%	36,708	3.75	95%	18,525	3.6	95%	19,730
	1	97%	1,890	1.17	92%	28,704	1.26	95%	15,675	0.95	95%	17,810
							0.4	93%	404,550	0.3	93%	382,500
xes	10%			Total 29%			46%					
V	−81M			7.4%								
R	9.6%						6.4%					

(After Yamazaki, 2008)

The results of this long-term effort have been a steadily increasing level of knowledge with respect to the resource potential of PN. Nevertheless, conclusions about the economic viability of PN exploitation are at best still imprecise and conflicting. Uncertainty with respect to economic viability is largely attributable to five factors:

1. Present analytical and economic inputs are based on prospecting and exploration data that are useful primarily for 'indicative' rather than the 'definitive"' economic analyses required for development and exploitation decisions.

2. All potential mining systems are presently prototypes developed for 'parameter setting' trial mining activities. Therefore many of the basic assumptions, such as the overall mining system and its capacity, efficiency and reliability are yet to be tested and proven.

3. Mining and processing technologies that impact directly on both the economics of PN exploitation and that of competing on-land deposits are rapidly evolving and have a high impact on economic viability.

4. Technological developments in related fields such as deep-sea oil and gas exploration and development, which are directly applicable to deep seabed mining, are rapidly evolving. These technological advances impact directly on mining feasibility, costs and project economics.

5. The extended timeframe of potential exploitation and the associated uncertainties with respect to supply, demand, markets and prices during that time make potential investment high-risk.

At present these above issues make it impossible to carry out, with the required high level of improved accuracy, a comprehensive economic analysis that would provide reliable information. Nevertheless, by imposing strong assumptions on the resources of the target area, the characteristics of mining technology and mineral processing methods and mineral markets, this kind of 'indicative' analysis continues. The most recent examples are the excellent work of the 2008 ISA 'Workshop on Polymetallic Nodule Mining Technology - Current Status and Challenges Ahead' held in Chennai, India (ISA, 2008a, b).

The Chennai workshop was specifically convened to develop a series of cost models for PN exploitation.[1] As reported by the ISA Secretary General Nii Odunton (2012) the workshop results showed that for a "... range of mining operations, from 1.2 to 3 million short tons per year for a 20-year mine life... incorporated into the model ... the internal rates of return for 12 alternative scenarios produced outcomes ranging from a low of 14.9 per cent to a high of 37.8 per cent ...."

The Chennai Workshop was of particular importance in that it provided an update of the ongoing and extensive research and development with respect to PN mining and processing. However, despite the extensive advances being made in mining and processing, the wide range of IRRs resulting from the 12 different scenarios highlighted in the Chennai Workshop reflect the continuing high degree of uncertainty still associated with PN exploitation programmes.

Sensitivity Analysis

However, past experience of on-land mining projects and previous and ongoing evaluations of potential PN projects all clearly demonstrate that exact IRR calculations during the early phases of project development are not as important as an understanding of the relative levels and change in the IRR resulting from changes in the main input variables.

Earlier work by the consultant on the economics of: a) PN in the Clarion Clipperton Zone; b) the Cook Islands nodules; c) cobalt crust in the Pacific; and d) marine polymetallic sulphide deposits of the Pacific Island nations shows that the main economic factors in rank order of importance (with 1 indicating the highest sensitivity), with respect to determining the economic viability of deep seabed deposits exploitation projects are the following main input variables:

1. Metal prices.
2. Metal content (type, amount, recovery).
3. Fiscal regime (national and international).
4. Processing costs (capital cost - type and commodities).
5. Mining costs (capital costs).
6. Energy/fuel costs.
7. Transportation costs.[2]

This sensitivity overview clearly defines a number of factors [3] that will influence the willingness of commercial operators to proceed with PN exploitation. Therefore, when metal prices are low, or potentially declining, investors are very conservative in terms of large capital investment in new, relatively high-risk mining ventures such as PN exploitation.

Although PN exploitation will take place within the administrative and fiscal regimes for exploitation defined by the ISA, it is important to note that at present the majority of potential developers, and most corporations, are closely linked with both their host governments and the global marketplace. Therefore there will almost always be concerns with respect to the political and economic risks of these linkages. For example, changes in national tax rates on corporations by their host governments or global economic recessions may have a direct or indirect impact. These risk variables will influence the required profit levels (IRR) of investments in the Area, which itself may already require an additional 5 to 10 per cent differential over an on-land development.

Notes

1. It should be emphasized that it is normally assumed that an internal rate of return of at least 30% would be required to make PN exploitation economically viable and competitive with on-land developments.

2. The IRR of PN developments is relatively insensitive to changes in transportation costs including both the shipment of nodules to the processing site and finished products to markets.

3. Inherent in the above are the underlying political, social and environmental risk factors that will have a direct or indirect impact

8. The Massive Nickel-Copper-Cobalt Sulphide to Nickel Laterite Transition

Introduction

For decades the future of deep seabed PN resource exploitation has largely been conditional on the extent to which PN exploitation, as measured by Return on Investment (ROI), equaled or surpassed that of on-land deposits producing similar commodities. Other major considerations, such as supply security (national and industrial), industry competitive advantage and resource and reserve availability were (and continue to be) important determinants. Local and international on-land mineral resource exploitation decisions are governed by the same factors. To date decisions about where to exploit have virtually all, except for a very limited amount of near shore mineral resource development, focused on onshore exploitation, with at least two important outcomes:

1. Industry driven onshore mineral exploitation has steadily and irrevocably moved from the exploitation of: a) large and high-grade sulphide deposits (Sudbury, Canada); to b) intermediate size and grade deposits; to c) to larger and lower grade deposits(the latter strongly resembling the PN resources of the Area).

2. The transition to larger and lower grade deposits required ever-increasing advances in mining and processing technology in order to capture the economies of scale required to make such deposits economically viable (particularly critical in terms of exploitation of resources such as PN).

Analysis of these factors shows that: a) mineral exploitation continues to be an evolutionary process, measured in decades rather than years; b) the transition is both technologically and economically driven; and c) economies of scale are critical for economic exploitation of large-scale, low-grade mineral resources. These three factors are critical to the timing and economic viability of PN exploitation, but more importantly for the study they may well significantly impact upon both proposed exploitation regulations and the fiscal regime that ISA may adopt.

Nickel-Cobalt Deposits

The world's primary production of nickel and cobalt comes from two types of mineral deposits, massive sulphide deposits (with associated high concentrations of copper) and laterite deposits (with little or no copper). Commercial production of New Caledonia's laterites began in 1875, and represented the world's largest source of nickel-cobalt until the production of Sudbury, Ontario's massive sulphide deposits beginning in 1905, followed by the development of the Norilsk deposit in Russia in the 1920s. Since the 1930s massive sulphide deposits of nickel-copper-cobalt have dominated global production.

Massive nickel-copper-cobalt sulphide deposits - The Russian Federation is presently the world's leading producer of nickel, with Russian mining giant Norilsk Nickel the world's largest producer, accounting for approximately one fifth of global production. Norilsk is the largest nickel sulphide deposit in the world. Canada is the world's second largest nickel producer with the majority of production coming from the Thompson Nickel Belt in Manitoba, Sudbury, Ontario, and the Ungava peninsula of Quebec. Australia is the world's third most important producer, from both sulphide and lateritic ores, of nickel. Massive nickel-copper-cobalt nickel sulphide deposits can occur as individual sulphide bodies but groups of deposits may occur in areas or belts that are tens, even hundreds of kilometers long.

The majority of today's nickel and cobalt, and a significant amount of copper, is produced from sulphide deposits largely because it is easier and cheaper, in terms of the cost of recovered metals, to mine and process than lateritic ore. However, known sulphide deposits are being depleted and large new discoveries are scarce.

Nickel Laterite Deposits

Nickel laterite deposits - It is estimated that about 70 per cent of current world land-based nickel resources are in laterite deposits - formed from the weathering (laterization) of ultramafic rocks, which strongly enriches the original nickel and cobalt content.

Nickel laterite deposits are typically of very large tonnage (in the range of 20 million to a billion tonnes) and of low grade, and located close to the surface. They tend to be tabular and flat, covering many square kilometers. Laterite deposits usually contain both an upper dark red limonite (higher in iron and lower in nickel, magnesium and silica) and a lower bright green saprolite zone (higher in nickel, magnesium and silica but lower in iron content). Due to the different quantities of iron, magnesium and silica in each zone they must be processed differently to cost-effectively retrieve the nickel and cobalt.

Laterite Development

Worldwide, the majority of nickel is still produced from sulphide sources. This is changing, however, with production from lateritic sources expected to rise to over 50 per cent by the end of 2012. This trend is the result of a combination of the relative availability of nickel laterites (approximately 70 per cent of land-based nickel resources) and the increasing use of hydrometallurgy for the extraction and recovery of metals. Since

nickel laterite ores will constitute the bulk of future nickel production, new laterite processing and development technologies are being aggressively developed and refined - particularly in terms of new integrated laterite development projects.

Processing Nickel Laterite Ores

Nickel laterites typically occur in regions favored by warm conditions with abundant rainfall, where prolonged weathering of ultramafic rocks (containing ferromagnesian minerals) has occurred. The result is a multi-layered residual concentration of weathered material high in nickel and cobalt. Traditionally, nickel and cobalt have been recovered from laterites by pyrometallurgical, hydrometallurgical or hybrid Pyro/Hydro metallurgical (the widely used 'Caron Process') means. The disadvantages of these processes include the requirement for higher-grade ores, substantial energy requirements and poor cobalt recoveries.

Pressure Acid Leaching - High Pressure Acid Leaching (HPAL) - Recently, various forms of pressure acid leaching (PAL) have been used, of which the most successful to date has been the High Pressure Acid Leaching (HAPL) system which is being rapidly adapted in the laterite nickel-cobalt mining industry. In the HPAL process, laterite ores are leached with sulfuric acid at high temperatures (240 to 270°) in titanium autoclaves. This process has the dual advantage of being applicable to widely differing types of ore and its high levels of both nickel and cobalt.

Atmospheric Pressure Acid Leaching APAL - APAL is basically the 'heap leaching' process that revolutionized the gold industry in the 1980s applied, with some modifications to laterite processing. APAL essentially requires that nickel-cobalt laterite ores be placed as a large mound ('heap') and the copper-nickel is extracted by leaching the heaped ore with acid. However, to date the APAL process has had low recovery rates of approximately 75 per cent nickel and 50 per cent cobalt.

In both of the above PAL processes, the

resulting 'leachate' is subsequently processed by solvent extraction. In the future, PAL processing may provide major breakthroughs in terms of processing low-grade lateritic ore. When that occurs, PAL processing promises to produce the following benefits that will collectively improve the economics of both lateritic and PN development:

1. Higher rates of metal recoveries at lower costs.

2. Easily filtered and environmentally stable.

3. Higher solution concentrations (and therefore smaller plant size).

Among the most promising, but at present somewhat uncertain technologies, is the HPAL process, which in the future may be particularly important to PN processing. The HPAL process is presently being used in four of the most recent nickel-cobalt projects. HPAL is fully implemented at the Goro Project in New Caledonia and the Ravensthorpe project in Australia, and is being used at the trialing stage at the Ambatovy project in Madagascar and the Ramu project in Papua New Guinea. However, there are a number of serious problems associated with HPAL that have raised questions as to its long-term viability for nickel-cobalt processing, which has had an impact on the whole nickel industry.

The extent of the growth in the nickel sector can be seen in a comparison of Table 14, showing the production of approximately 258 kt of laterite nickel from 16 developments, while new and projected increases in laterite nickel production from existing operations are expected to result in a net change in productive capacity of over 400 kt by 2014 (Table15). Although it is highly doubtful, for a range of reasons, that all or most of the planned developments in Table 15 will happen, it is very clear that the long-term supply of nickel, and therefore that of its associated cobalt is not in doubt in the short to intermediate term.

Table 14:   Nickel laterite mines, processing configuration and companies (2008 data)

Project, Country	Ore kt	% Ni	%Co	kt Ni	T/Co	Process	Company
Sorowako, Indonesia	4675	2.10	-	72.4	-	RKEF	Vale Inco/Pt Inco
Doniambo, New Caledonia	2930	2.0	-	51.1	-	RKEF	SLN/Eramet
Cerro Matoso, Colombia	~2415	~2.3	-	41.6	-	RKEF	BHP Billiton
Yabulu, Australia	-	-	-	35.1	1600	Caron	BHP Billiton
Moa Bay, Cuba	2881	~1.5	~0.16	32.4	3428	HPAL	Sherritt International
Murrin Murrin, Australia	2446	1.43	~0.10	30.5	2018	HPAL	Minara Resources
Larco-Larymna, Greece	2500	1.2	-	21.2	-	RKEF	Larco SA
Falcondo, Dominican Republic	1708	1.14	-	18.8	-	RKEF	Xstrata
Pomalaa, Indonesia	1113	1.58	-	17.6	-	RKEF	PT Antam
Kavadarci, Macedonia	~750	~2	-	15.0	-	RKEF	Feni Industries /Cunico
Loma de iquel, Venezuela	677	1.6	-	10.9	-	RKEF	Anglo American

Project, Country	Ore kt	% Ni	%Co	kt Ni	T/Co	Process	Company
Rio Tuba (Coral Bay), Philippines	858	1.5	-	9.7	-	HPAL	Sumitomo JV
Codemin, Brazil	476	2.1	-	9.1	-	RKEF	Anglo American
Ufaleynickel, Russian Federation	-	-	-	~9	-	RKEF	OAO Ufaleynickel
Berong, Philippines	~293	~1.48	-	4.3	-	Caron	Toledo Mining
Cawse, Australia	678	0.69	nd	3.7	-	HAPL	Norilsk Nickel
Total laterite (Caron)	>293	~1.48	-	>35.1	>1600		
Total laterite (HPAL)	~6900	~1.4	~0.12	76.3	>5500		
Total laterite (RKEF)	~17,250	~1.0	-	257.7	-		

Note: Data is derived from respective company annual reports or websites, additional data sourced from NRC (var.), USGS, and '-' denotes no data; 'RKEF' denotes rotary kiln electric furnace.

Table 15:   New and major expansions to nickel mines, 2011-14 (units kt)

Mine	Country	Deposit Type	Net Capacity Change	2011	2012	2013	2014
Philippines Ore	Philippines	Laterite	64	110	158	173	174
Onca-Puma	Brazil	Laterite	44	8	22	39	52
Ambatovy	Madagascar	Laterite	42	0	12	28	42
Ravensthorpe	Australia	Laterite	30	6	17	30	36
Barro Alto	Brazil	Laterite	29	18	33	41	47
Antam High Grade	Indonesia	Laterite	29	48	69	73	77
Goro	New Caledonia	Laterite	28	9	16	27	37
Koniambo	New Caledonia	Laterite	26	0	0	16	26
Santa Rita	Brazil	Laterite	8	16	20	24	24
Cerro Matoso - Montelibano	Colombia	Laterite	16	44	60	60	60
Taguang	Myanmar	Laterite	16	0	2	11	16
SLN - Garnierite	Indonesia	Laterite	13	57	62	65	70
Indept & SLN Ore - Garnierite	Indonesia	Laterite	10	32	35	41	42
Kevitsa	Finland	Laterite	10	0	3	8	10
Phoenix	Botswana	Sulphide	10	9	19	19	19
Nkomati	South Africa	Sulphide	8	11	13	17	20
Talvivaara	Finland	Sulphide	20	30	40	45	50

In one of many examples, Koniambo Nickel SAS of New Caledonia is presently completing construction of a world-class industrial complex for the exploitation of the Koniambo nickel laterite deposit. This unexploited ore body currently comprises 142.1 million tonnes of measured and indicated saprolite resources with a 2.13 per cent nickel content, 140.7 million tonnes of inferred saprolite resources with a 2.16 per cent nickel content and 104 million tonnes of inferred limonite resources with a 1.50 per cent nickel content.

Present plans envisage 25 years of mining operations, at an annual production of 60 kt/year, with a strong possibility of additional resources that will make it possible to extend the life of the mine and the production of ore to over 50 years.

Nickel Resources

Sulphide deposits are being used up at a faster rate than they are being replenished and the quantity of sulphide-bearing ores is declining as are the grades of the remaining ores.

As a result almost 20 per cent of new sulphide production primarily from smaller sulphide discoveries will represent replacement feed.

It is anticipated that future nickel supply will be derived primarily from newly developing laterite ore bodies; especially limonite deposits that can be processed by technically complex and operationally demanding HPAL technology. Although there are a sufficient number of committed new nickel projects to meet demand over the next 5 years, a major delay in just one of the large HPAL projects could leave the nickel industry supply constrained until well into the next decade. In summary:

1. Supply and demand are evenly matched in next 5 years.

2. Greenfield / Brownfield projects (committed) 440,000 tpa.

3. Closures / fall in output due to declining ore grades - 50,000 tpa.

4. Total increase in supply of primary nickel - 370,000 tpa.

5. Increase in consumption of primary nickel - 325,000 tpa.

6. Total increase in demand for primary nickel - 355,000 tpa.

9. Recovering 'Lost Benefits': Corporate Social Responsibility

Issues

It is recognized that under UNCLOS and the CHM concept the ISA is to recover resource rents from PN exploitation and part of these resource rents will be apportioned to developing nations - by a yet to be determined formula and process. At one level this would appear to closely follow normal land-based exploitation where the resource rents accrue to the government for use in national development. However, when this concept is applied to PN exploitation there is one very major difference. Specifically, PN exploitation activity (principally mining and concentration) is spatially isolated (being in the Area) and therefore does not <u>directly</u> impact upon individual stakeholders, communities or national economies. The result is that:

1. No actual in-country expenditures will accrue to developing nations but rather primarily to developed nations, the present 'stakeholders' of potential mining areas.

2. The 'multiplier effect' of resource exploitation in terms of economic development and diversification, infrastructure, health, education and welfare are essentially 'lost benefits'.

3. Direct corporate expenditures normally devoted to 'mine and development'-related social programmes, and often directed towards ensuring long-term sustainability benefits, will not be spent and are therefore another 'lost benefit'.

Importantly, from a historical perspective, nations have struggled to achieve sustainable development from resource exploitation. This has led to the relatively recent practice of nations requiring mine site and regional community development through development funds, social development plans and strengthening and diversifying local economies in an effort to ensure that when a mine closes there is something sustainable left behind. So it is a concern that the primary method envisaged to benefit developing countries is with money, which, from a historical perspective, has not often contributed to sustainable development. This would appear to place a far greater emphasis on what to do with the funds. For example, should a proportion of the fiscal returns be invested into education relating to marine environmental study? Such an idea would be in concert with the corporate social responsibility (CSR) activities that are also being contemplated, such as training, in an attempt to capture the 'lost benefits'.[1]

For a range of political, economic, social and practical reasons it is in the best interest of the ISA and of potential exploiters of the PN of the Area to directly address the issue of 'lost benefits' in the regulatory and fiscal regimes of PN exploitation.

Corporate Social Responsibility

CSR is the way companies manage their businesses to make a positive impact on society through economic, environmental and social action. On land governments have historically arbitrated the relationship between society, business and industry and have viewed CSR as compliance with the laws and regulations. To a larger or smaller degree this may well be the relationship between the ISA and potential PN exploiters. However, although regulation can have significant social value, companies normally view them simply as a cost of doing business and a means of avoiding litigation. Nevertheless many industries, including mining sector corporations, have recognized that compliance with laws and regulations is not sufficient and that they need to be far more environmentally, socially, economically and culturally responsible by adopting and expanding CSR obligations. Indeed, a surprising number of companies regard CSR as a necessity for growth and differentiation as shown by a recent survey by IBM (2012) that found:

1. Over two-thirds (68 per cent) of business leaders surveyed are focusing on CSR activities to create new revenue streams.

2. Over half (54 per cent) believe that their companies' CSR activities are already giving them an advantage over their top competitors.

A Possible Solution

The widespread expansion of the CSR concept has led to the creation of the new 'Hybrid Social Business' (HSB) model. The HSB model is a significant modification of the traditional business model, which only incorporated general levels of CSR. A HSB company explicitly sets the expectation that it will simultaneously pursue two objectives: a) specific positive social impacts and returns; and b) specific baseline financial returns. In this respect it differs from the more pure Social Business Model of Yunus (2010) and others focused primarily on non-profit industries.

The HSB model may be of particular interest

to the ISA in terms of addressing the 'lost benefits' issue:

1. The concept explicitly address the 'dual challenge' issue in that the corporation will fund and assist specific programmes of value to all mankind, for example the sustainable development of deep seabed resources to preserve the marine environment and to reduce poverty while meeting the ROI requirements of investors.

2. The HSB model is directly applicable to supporting the extant International Seabed Authority Endowment Fund for Collaborative Marine Scientific Research on the International Seabed (MSR) programme (ISA, 2008a,b).

3. From a market perspective an HSB company programme has significant appeal to many potential investors and shareholders (particularly diversified portfolio investors) who wish to invest in socially responsible corporations.

Conclusion

Linking HSB and MSR with issues directly relevant to the Area, and with developing nation's local, national and coastal management activities, represents a win-win opportunity for the ISA, industry and developing nations, and it is strongly recommended that ISA address this issue as part of both the regulatory and fiscal regime for PN exploitation.

Notes

[1.] To some extent the amount of funding is less important than the reality of specifically addressing the issue of both 'lost benefits' and the issue of demonstrable CSR.

10.   Conclusions and Recommendations

The key roles, functions and organizational structures of the ISA, in terms of managing the development and exploitation of PN resources in the Area, are clearly identified in UNCLOS, Annex III and the Agreement on the Implementation of Part XI, and are well summarized by Lodge (2001a, 2001b and 2012). The key overarching issues related to the management of the commercial exploitation of PN, which will be equally applicable in most cases to polymetallic sulphide and cobalt-rich ferromanganese crust exploitation, have been detailed in the preceding discussions. This elaboration of issues has defined a number of specific issues and actions that the ISA will need to address as it proceeds with the management of exploration and exploitation of the metal resources of the Area. There follows a brief outline for a proposed strategy of 'preparing for exploitation', followed by an evaluation of specific issues of importance pertaining to the role of the ISA in its administration of PN exploitation in the Area. This is followed by an assessment of areas for future research and study.

Preparing for Exploitation

The potential for PN, polymetallic sulphide and cobalt-rich manganese crust exploitation within the Area is arguably higher now than ever before. This impending reality requires that the ISA, as essentially the 'Mining Ministry of the Area', must rapidly prepare to meet this evolving challenge.

Table 16:   Strategic plan for formulation of a Regulatory Regime for PN

Timing	Recommended Activity
2013	Preparation of PN Regulatory Regime White Paper as background for Conference on PN Exploitation Regulatory Regime and Stakeholder Survey. White paper, Conference and Stakeholder Survey to include topics including: • Comparative regulatory regimes relevant to PN exploitation. • Comparative organizational and administrative arrangements relevant to PN exploitation. • Pre-feasibility and feasibility study components. • Plans of Work for Exploitation. • PN Exploitation and Environment (Environmental Management and Monitoring Plans). • ISA Assessment and Monitoring Methodologies.
2014	Conference and Stakeholder Survey
	Stakeholder Survey response analysis
	Small working groups convene on selected topics
	Publication of Proceedings, Stakeholder Survey and Responses
	Small working groups issue recommendations
	Economic sensitivity study for 'User pays' fees and costs
	PN exploitation regulations drafted by ISA Legal and Technical Commission

Timing	Recommended Activity
	Study on ISA institutional strengthening and capacity development for exploitation-cadastre, compliance, monitoring, inspection and enforcement functions
2015	Expert/stakeholder consultations on draft PN exploitation regulations
	Revision of draft regulations by ISA Legal and Technical Commission
	Consideration by ISA Council
	Promulgation
	Implementation of recommendations from institutional strengthening and capacity development study
2016	First applications received for provisional PN exploitation licences

This will require the development of a strategic framework that allows the ISA to put in place the necessary mandates, organizational capacities (technical and administrative), policies and regulations (implementing rules and regulations) and capacities (fiscal, manpower and specialties). Central to these measures is the need to establish on overall strategy (Table 18) against which to measure progress and preparedness. The following is an attempt to broadly identify the major building blocks that must be developed over the next 3 to 5 years to ensure that the ISA can meet the challenge.

Specific Issues

Organizational - It is possible, depending on the scope of PN exploitation that takes place, that the existing structure of the ISA may be able to meet the added requirement of 'shepherding' a limited number of exploitation activities. However, should exploration and exploitation activities increase dramatically, as seems possible in light of recent increases in licence applications and the approaching deadline for many operators to apply for exploitation licences, existing ISA capacity may well be inadequate and therefore it is recommended that:

1. The ISA consider the development of an internal Mining Inspectorate with the specific responsibilities of maintaining oversight and compliance with all exploration and exploitation licence activities. This would specifically include a 'Mining Registry', a 'Compliance Office', a 'Data and Archive Center' and an

'Inspector General's Office'. There are many different administrative models but for efficiency, capacity and security a separate operating unit would be advisable. Such a responsible agency does not presently exist within the ISA, which in accordance with the evolutionary approach to its establishment reflected in the 1994 Agreement, has been principally operating as an international organization providing meeting services to member States and expert bodies. However, the present high level of interest, coupled with the need for many operators to apply for exploitation licences by 2016, indicates a critical need to begin detailed discussions for the funding, planning and implementation of such an 'administrative agency' capacity within the ISA in the near future. In addressing this need it is recommended that the ISA undertake a comparative analysis of representative 'administrative agencies' as a basis for the development of a similar capacity within the ISA. This capacity would need to include transparent funding mechanisms (on a cost-recovery or alternative basis), secure data management and analysis, maintenance of a mining claims registry to international standards (ISO 4001) and financial and accounting capacity.

In addition to these major proposed structural changes in preparation for PN exploitation, there should be a similar organizational change with respect to environmental activities, which are both recognized and partially underway, and which the consultant believes should be more formally defined:

2. The ISA should form a permanent committee to address the clear and urgent need to rationalize and incorporate past and present environmental rules, regulations and requirements with, and within, the evolving exploitation frameworks for PN and other metal resources within the Area. This is logically an LTC function but there needs to be transparent engagement with the deep-sea mining industry and other stakeholders in this process. The real concern is that: a) this process is not viewed as an ad hoc activity but as a critical component of whatever 'responsible agency' ensues; b) working groups and committees serve as a defined interface for environmental regulations for both prospecting and exploitation; c) there is a 'competent' body providing continuity across differing resources (polymetallic nodules, polymetallic sulphides and cobalt-rich crusts, d) the process identifies and addresses environmental issues as they might arise and e) the process would become a permanent part of the 'responsible agency'. More importantly, it is argued that it would benefit the ISA if industry recognizes that there is a formal, continuing and identified group monitoring their activities.

Finally, and closely linked with b) above, as the ISA moves towards a much broader spectrum of activities with respect to prospecting, exploration and exploitation of nodules, cobalt-rich manganese crusts and polymetallic sulphide deposits within the Area, the consultant recommends:

3. That the ISA undertake a study specific to the development of a set of unified and common operating procedures (as is done within most on-land mining ministries and agencies), for the evaluation, licensing and monitoring of PN, cobalt-rich manganese crusts and polymetallic sulphides prospecting, exploration and exploitation.

Regulatory - The ISA should develop and put in place a 'staged' or 'phased' provisional licensing system requiring that, prior to the expiration of an exploration licence, contractors interested in proceeding to the mining phase must first apply for a *provisional mining licence based upon preparation and submission of a pre-feasibility study and work plans to undertake a detailed bankable feasibility study based upon a pilot PN mining operation in the contract area.*

Fiscal Issues - It is anticipated that fiscal issues, in particular resource rents, will continue to be of major and increasing importance as exploitation activities within the Area advance, and regardless of the mechanism chosen, it will almost certainly not be universally acceptable or adequate to meet the expectations of all recipient member countries.

Therefore it is recommended that the ISA pay particular attention to the following:

4. Ensure that whatever resource rent process is employed is:
   a. Simple.
   b. Equitable.
   c. Transparent.
   d. Defensible.
   e. Response to change.

5. The issues of 'deductible expenditure', credit and financing of projects and tax benefits should be closely monitored to ensure that: a) the ISA receives its fair share of 'resource rents' after deductions; and b) host country commercial policies do not give an unfair advantage to the commercial exploiter of the resources.

6. The ISA should closely monitor the 'transactional' portion of the mineral processing part of the 'mine to market' chain to ensure that all transactions are 'arm's length' and closely reflect prevailing market prices for metals.

This will be particularly critical with respect to any royalty-based resource rent capture scheme ultimately adopted.

Future Research and Study

The present study has identified a number of specific actions and areas of specific research and study that should be considered in preparation for the development and implementation of a fiscal and legal regime for the management and exploitation of PN and other metal resources in the Area. The consultant believes that among the most important recommendations are:

1. The development over the next 3 to 5 years of a framework of activities for the ISA, in conjunction with potential PN developers[1] and member countries, that will put in place the internal ISA structure and capacity to manage PN exploitation in the Area.

2. Conduct a component analysis of a tax-like infrastructure (incorporating rules, procedures and administrative staff, audits and legal decisions) for determining project profits and ensuring that optimum resource development and financial flows are achieved.

3. Undertake a cost-benefit analysis to determine the sensitivity levels for fees and costs associated with PN

4. An evaluation by tax professionals, with international experience and knowledge of the special characteristics of mining, of the need for and applicability of the development by ISA of a business tax code infrastructure for PN development within the Area.

5. Undertake framework studies specific to the following areas of PN exploitation activities:

    a. Monitoring and compliance.
    b. Resource recovery, utilization and valuation.
    c. Creation of implementing rules and regulations for legal regime.
    d. Structure of an Environmental Mining Plan.

6. Definitional meetings to reach concurrence on the structure and requirements for:

    a. Pilot mining.
    b. Prefeasibility metrics.
    c. Classification of resources and reserves specific to seabed mining.

Notes

[1] As noted, for purpose of this report, the consultant initially stated that they are viewed as "private sector companies incorporated under the laws of their respective nations."

Bibliography

Barclays Commodity Research, 2012, Metal Magnifier-Supply Development (July), Barclays Bank PLC, London, England, 72p.

Charles, C., et al., 1990, Views on future nodule technologies based on IFREMER-GEMONOD studies. Materials Society 14(3/4), pp.299-326.

Cordes, John A., 1995, 'An Introduction to the Taxation of Mineral Rents' in *the Taxation of Mineral Enterprises*, ed. James Otto,: Graham Trotman, London, pp.25-46.

Crundwell, M.M., Moats, Ramachandran, V., Robinson, T.G., and Davenport, W.G., 2011, Extractive metallurgy of nickel, cobalt and platinum group metals, Elsivier, Ltd. Amsterdam, Netherlands, 609p.

CPM, 2012, Manganese market outlook, CPM Group, New York, 20p.

CPM, 2011, CPM electrolytic manganese long-term outlook, CPM Group, New York, 160p, http://www.researchandmarkets.com/reports/2069257/cpm_electrolytic_manganese_longterm_market

Fisher, K.G., 2011, Cobalt Processing Developments, Southern African Institute of Mining and Metallurgy, 6th Southern African Base Metals Conference, pp. 237-258.

Frakes, Jennifer, 2003, 'The Common Heritage of Mankind Principle and the Deep Seabed, Outer Space, and Antarctica: Will Developed and Developing Nations Reach a Compromise?', Wisconsin International Law Journal 21: 409, 25p.

Government of Western Australia, 1994, Offshore Minerals Act of 1994, Government of Western Australia, 267p, http://www.comlaw.gov.au/Details/C2004C00450

Hein, J., 2012, Prospects for rare earth elements from marine minerals, ISA Briefing Paper 02/12, International Seabed Authority, Kingston Jamaica, 4p.

Hilman, C. T. and Gosling, B. B.,1985, Mining deep ocean manganese nodules: description and economic analysis of a potential venture, IC9015. US: Bureau of Mines, 19p.

IBM, 2012, Attaining sustainable growth through corporate social responsibility, IBM Institute for Business Value, New York, 17p, http://www-935.ibm.com/services/us/gbs/bus/pdf/ibv-gbe03019-usen-00-csr.pdf

ISA, 2000, Regulations on prospecting and exploration for polymetallic nodules in the Area, 21p, http://www.isa.org.jm/files/documents/EN/Regs/MiningCode.pdf

ISA, 2010, A geologic model of polymetallic nodule deposits in the Clarion-Clipperton Fracture zone, Technical Study 6, International Seabed Authority, Kingston, Jamaica, 105pp, http://www.isa.org.jm/files/documents/EN/Pubs/GeoMod-web.

ISA, 2011, Environmental management needs for exploration and exploitation of deep sea minerals, ISA Technical Study No. 10, International Seabed Authority, Kingston Jamaica, 48p, http://www.isa.org.jm/files/documents/EN/Pubs/TS10/TS10-Final.pdf

ISA, 2008, International Seabed Authority Endowment Fund: Collaborative Marine Scientific Research, International Seabed Authority, Kingston, Jamaica, 12p, http://www.isa.org.jm/files/documents/EN/efund/FactSheet-rev1.pdf

ISA, 2008a, Report on the International Seabed Authorities Workshop on Polymetallic Nodule Mining Technology - Current Status and Challenges Ahead, ISBA/14/LTC/3, International Seabed Authority, Kingston, Jamaica, 4p, http://www.isa.org.jm/files/documents/EN/14Sess/LTC/ISBA-14LTC-3.pdf

ISA, 2008b, Background Document, Workshop on Polymetallic Nodule Mining Technology - Current Status and Challenges Ahead, International Seabed Authority, Kingston, Jamaica, 18p, http://www.isa.org.jm/files/documents/EN/Workshops/Feb2008/Backgrd.pdf

ISA, 2012, Seabed Council debates report of finance committee on Authority's 2013-2014 budget; approves work plan for Exploitation Code; proposes Odunton for re-election as Secretary-General, Press Release SB/18/13, International Seabed Authority, Kingston, Jamaica, 9p.

Lodge, M., 2001a, The International Seabed Authority's Regulations on Prospecting and Exploration for Polymetallic Nodules in the Area, *The Journal*, V 10 Article 2, Centre for Energy, Petroleum and Mineral Law and Policy, Dundee, Scotland, 29p, http://www.dundee.ac.uk/cepmlp/journal/html/vol10/article10-2.htmlz

Lodge, M., 2001b, The regulatory regime for deep seabed mining, Proceedings of the Seminar on prospecting, exploration and exploitation of deep seabed mineral resources: challenges for the Caribbean and opportunities for collaboration, International Seabed Authority, Kingston Jamaica, http://www.isa.org.jm/files/documents/EN/Seminars/2011/RegulatoryRegime-MLodge.pdf

Lodge, M. 2008a, Collaborative Marine Scientific Research on the International Seabed, *Journal of Ocean Technology*, pp.30-36.

Lodge, M., 2012, Observations on the structure and functions of the organs of the Authority, ISA Sensitization Seminar, United Nations, New York, 32p, http://www.isa.org.jm/files/documents/EN/Seminars/2012/Michael.pdf

Morgan, C., 2012, A geological model of polymetallic nodule deposits in the Clarion-Clipperton fracture zone, ISA Briefing Paper 1/12, International Seabed Authority, Kingston Jamaica, 12p.

Mukhopadhyay, R., Gosh, A.K, and. Iyer, S.D. (2008), The Indian Ocean nodule field: geology and resource potential, Elsivier, London, 25p.

MMDA, 2011, Model Mine Development Agreement, International Bar Association, London, England, 192p.

Nautilus Minerals, 2011, Solawara 1 Project - high grade copper and gold, Nautilus Mining Company, Toronto, Canada, 2p. http://www.nautilusminerals.com/s/Projects-Solwara.asp

Nethery, B, 2003., 'The Role of Feasibility Studies in Mining Ventures', Presentation to Conference Board of Canada, Structuring More Effective Mining Ventures, Feb. 17 and 18, 2003, Vancouver, B.C., http://www.cartaexploration.com/downloads/external%20pdfs/

Otto, J., Andrews, C., Cawood, F., Guj, F., Stermole, F., and Tilton, J., 2006, Impact of royalties on a mine: quantitative analysis, Chapter 4 in 'Mining royalties: a global study of their impact on investors, government and civil society', World Bank, Washington, D.C.

Otto et al., 2006, Mining Royalties: A Global Study of Their Impact on Investors, Government, and Civil Society, World Bank, Washington, D.C..

Price, Waterhouse, Coopers, 2009, Price Waterhouse Coopers; Effective Rate Comparison of Global Mining Industry 2008, London, England, 8p.

Randhawa, N. S., Jana, R. K, and Das N, 2012, Manganese nodules residue: potential raw material for FeSiMn, *International Journal of Metallurgical Engineering* 1(2), Rosemead, California, pp.22-27, http://article.sapub.org/10.5923.j.ijmee.20120102.03.html

Soreide, F, Lund, F, and Markussen, J.M., 2001, Deep ocean mining reconsidered - a study of the manganese nodules deposits in the Cook Islands, Proceedings of the fourth ocean mining symposium. Szczecin, Poland, p.88-93.

United Nations, 1982, United Nations Convention on the Law of the Sea (UNCLOS), United Nations, New York, http://www.un.org/Depts/los/convention_agreements/texts/unclos/closindx.htm

United Nations, 1994, Agreement relating to the Implementation of Part XI of the United Nations Convention on the Law of the Sea of 10 December 1994,
http://www.un.org/Depts/los/convention_agreements/texts/unclos/closindx.htm

USGS/USBM, 1980, Principles of a resource/reserve classification for minerals, Geological Survey Circular 831, United States Geological Survey, Reston, Virginia, 11p,
http://pubs.usgs.gov/circ/1980/0831/report.pdf

USGS, 2012a, Mineral commodity summaries 2012, United States Geological Survey, Reston, Virginia, 198p,
http://minerals.usgs.gov/minerals/pubs/mcs/2012/mcs2012.pdf

USGS, 2012b, Mineral industry surveys United States Geological Survey, Reston, Virginia
http://minerals.usgs.gov/minerals/pubs/commodity/mis.html

Wilburn, D.R., 2011, Cobalt mineral exploration and supply from 1995 through 2013, US Geological Survey Scientific Investigation report 2011-5084, Washington, D.C. 18p.

Yamazaki, T, 2008, Model mining units of the 20th century and the economics (production requirements, area requirements and vertical integration), Workshop on Polymetallic Nodule Mining Technology - Current Status and Challenges Ahead, International Seabed Authority, Kingston, Jamaica, 9p,
http://www.isa.org.jm/files/documents/EN/Workshops/Feb2008/Yamazaki-Abst.pdf

Yunus, Muhammad, 2009, Creating a World Without Poverty: Social Business and the Future of Capitalism, Public Affairs, 320p.

Yunus, Muhammad, 2010, Building Social Business: The New Kind of Capitalism That Serves Humanity's Most Pressing Needs, Public Affairs, New York, 226p.

World Bank, 2012, Model Community Development Framework for the mining sector program, World Bank, Washington, D.C.,
http://web.worldbank.org/WBSITE/EXTERNAL/TOPICS/EXTOGMC/0,,contentMDK:22616285~pagePK:210058~piPK:210062~theSitePK:336930,00.html

WTO, 2012, Dispute settlement DS394: China - Measures Related to the Exportation of Various Raw Materials, World Trade Organization, Geneva, Switzerland.